SABRINA FISHER REECE

God is Not A Man

Rediscovering the Divine Balance of Masculine and Feminine Within Us All

This book is for the seeker who loves God deeply but knows there is more to understand. It is for the man learning that strength includes tenderness, and the woman who has always sensed she was never spiritually secondary. May these pages widen your view of the divine and remind you that the presence you call God has always been larger, closer, and more inclusive than you were taught.

–Bri Reece

Contents

Introduction

Breaking the Box Without Breaking Faith

For most of our lives, many of us have been taught to imagine God as male. We pray to "Our Father." We refer to God as He. Authority is often pictured in masculine form because that is the language we inherited. That image has been repeated for generations, wrapped in tradition, reinforced in sermons, embedded in scripture readings, and spoken in prayer. For many, it feels familiar and comforting. It represents order, protection, and structure.

Yet for others, something about that singular image feels incomplete. It can seem as though an entire dimension of divine expression has been left unacknowledged. When God is consistently described in masculine terms alone, the feminine reflection within creation can feel overlooked or diminished. If both male and female were created in the image of God, then reducing the divine to one side of that design invites a deeper question. That question is precisely what this book is willing to explore.

This book is not written to tear down tradition. It is written to expand it and offer a broader perspective. There is a meaningful difference between rejecting faith and deepening your understanding of it. I love God and acknowledge all that God has done in my life. At the same time, it is only honest to admit that I was never given a choice about what religion I would follow, or whether I would follow one at all. A child who is two or three years old and taken to church is not making a spiritual decision. That choice is made for them.

I am not resentful in any way. In fact, I am eternally grateful to my grandmother for raising me in the church. That foundation protected me during vulnerable seasons and gave me structure when I needed it most. Still, gratitude does not eliminate the importance of personal choice and discovery. There comes a point in adulthood when faith must become chosen rather than inherited.

I believe it is important to search for God in a way that feels intentional and personal. Travel if you can. Visit different countries. Sit in on book studies. Listen to other perspectives. Observe how people across cultures honor the divine. Then ask yourself honestly whether, as an adult, you would still choose the same path your parents or grandparents chose for you. Find your own path.

Growth does not have to mean rebellion, and questioning does not equal disrespect. Sometimes growth simply means allowing yourself to ask whether what you were given was the full picture or only part of it. Mature faith can withstand inquiry. It does not collapse under honest examination. Questions about God should not be dismissed or silenced. We are living in an age where "just trust God" or "just go pray about it" is no longer enough for many sincere seekers. Faith must become personal, not just inherited.

Each of us must search individually to discover our own understanding of God, and that journey deserves respect. Different paths do not automatically mean different levels of devotion. They often reflect different stages of growth, culture, and experience. When someone chooses to explore their faith more deeply, that exploration should not be treated as betrayal. It should be seen as maturity and it should be encouraged.

I was raised in the Church of God in Christ, and I am deeply grateful for that foundation. It gave me structure, discipline, and a reverence for God that has never left me. However, as I grew older and began researching and seeking God for myself, I realized that I carried many unanswered questions. Those questions were not born out of rebellion. They were born out of a genuine desire to understand the fullness of the divine.

If God is infinite, omnipresent, and the creator of all that exists, then limiting that divine source to one gender becomes difficult to reconcile. Infinity cannot be contained inside a single human category. When we open the first chapter of Genesis, we read that humanity was created in the image of God. Humanity consist of male and female. So that statement alone invites reflection. It does not say that only men carry God's divine image or imprint. It includes both. All of us are made in the image of God.

For centuries, societies were structured through patriarchy. Leadership, governance, and spiritual authority were largely male dominated. Language reflected that structure. When divine authority was described, masculine terms became the norm. Over time, metaphor solidified into assumption. What may have begun as relational language slowly hardened into literal belief.

None of that means faith was wrong. It means culture and theology evolved together, as they always do.

The divine source I choose to call God is not an old man seated in the sky keeping score. That image may have served a psychological purpose in certain eras, but it cannot contain omnipotence. The presence that animates life is far more expansive than any human portrait.

Consider something simple. You do not command your heart to beat. You do not consciously direct oxygen into your bloodstream. You do not tell your skin how to heal when it is cut. There is no doubt a higher intelligence operating within you every moment without your instruction. Cells regenerate. Blood circulates. Breath moves in and out while you sleep. Something sustains that order and it is not you.

Whether someone calls that intelligence God, Source, Yahweh, Elohim, Creator, or Universe does not alter its function. The name is secondary.

The presence is constant and undeniable.

What becomes more difficult to defend is the idea that such an all encompassing presence would be exclusively male. Creation itself expresses polarity. Strength and softness. Logic and intuition. Structure and flow. Initiative and receptivity etc. If the created world reflects dual expression, the creator must contain the fullness of what is expressed.

Each human being carries both masculine and feminine energy. Biology does not erase energetic balance. Some individuals operate more comfortably in one expression than the other, and culture often rewards one while criticizing the other. Men can be shamed for tenderness. Women can be criticized for authority. Yet imbalance is not identity. It is simply imbalance.

This book is written for the seeker who senses that divine reality is larger than inherited images. It is for the believer who still prays, still honors God, but knows that reverence does not require confinement. It is for the person who has outgrown fear based interpretations without losing spiritual devotion.

Many ideas that are labeled modern spirituality are, in truth, rediscovered wisdom. I collect books from the nineteenth and early twentieth centuries that speak openly about imagination shaping reality, about belief influencing experience, about divine law responding to thought. Meditation, sound, affirmation, manifestation, inner kingdom consciousness, none of these are new inventions. Humanity has always known that there is creative power within.

If scripture teaches that the kingdom of heaven is within us, then divine presence is not far away. It is not distant or confined to some far-off realm. It is not separated from humanity. It operates through human life. It is active within both men and women. It moves through us, works through us, and lives within both men and women. A presence shared by both cannot be limited to one. If the divine dwells in both, then it must be greater than either category alone.

Expanding our understanding of God does not weaken faith. It strengthens it. It restores dignity where hierarchy once existed. It dissolves the quiet implication that one gender stands closer to divine image than the other. It invites balance instead of division.

You are not required to abandon your upbringing to explore this conversation. You are not required to reject tradition or scripture. The only requirement is openness. A willingness to consider that infinity may be greater than the frame we placed around it.

By the time you finish this book, my hope is not that you argue theology with anyone. My hope is that you feel relief. Relief that you no longer have to reconcile omnipotence with limitation. Relief that you no longer have to silently question where women fit into divine image. Relief that you can embrace both strength and softness within yourself without confusion.

If God created male and female, then divine source contains both.

Understanding that is not rebellion. It is remembrance.

1

The Image We Inherited

Before we question an image, we have to understand how it was formed. Most of us did not consciously choose the way we picture God. The image was handed down to us through sermons, prayers, paintings, ancestral history, hymns, and the language of those who came before us. It arrived early in childhood and settled quietly into our imagination before we were even old enough to evaluate it.

The language of "Father" became central in many religious traditions, especially within Christianity. That word carried authority, provision, protection, and governance. In ancient societies, fathers were heads of households. Kings were male. Priests and Popes were male. Leadership and divinity were closely intertwined in cultural understanding. When spiritual language developed, it naturally reflected the social order of its time.

None of this means faith was wrong or misguided. It simply means that theology did not develop in separate from culture. Human beings use the language taught to them and available to them from whoever raised them.

When describing something as vast and incomprehensible as God, the amazing divine source that created us all, metaphor becomes necessary. The problem arises when metaphor hardens into literal limitation.

Referring to God as Father was relational and conversational language delivered as fact. It created familiarity for us. It provided emotional context which we needed at the time. It gave people a framework for understanding care and authority. Yet a framework is not the full structure itself. When we forget that language is symbolic, we risk mistaking description for permanent definition.

Scripture itself contains many complexities. In Isaiah, God is described as a mother comforting her child. In Genesis, humanity is declared to be created in the image of God, male and female. Even within the sacred texts, there are glimpses of divine qualities that extend beyond masculine imagery. Those passages often receive less emphasis, not because they are absent, but because tradition selected which metaphors to amplify.

Over time, repetition shapes perception that is normal. When a congregation hears "He" thousands of times in prayer, imagination forms around that pronoun. Paintings of male Gods reinforce it. The biblical stories also reinforce it. Cultural hierarchy reinforces it. Eventually the image feels unquestionable, not because it is the only possibility, but because it is the most familiar one.

Familiarity is powerful because it feels safe and I completely understand that. When we grow up believing something, it becomes part of how we see ourselves and the world. It effect all of the concepts we feel strongly about and it shapes our entire and belief system. Challenging that familiarity can feel unsettling, almost like questioning a piece of your identity. For many believers, even asking whether God is exclusively male can feel uncomfortable, as if the question itself crosses a line or betrays God in some way.

But asking a question should not be viewed as betrayal or dishonor.

Questions are a natural part of growth. In fact, sincere inquiry can be an act of reverence when it comes from a desire to understand God more fully rather than from rebellion.

The time for blind, un-examined faith should pass. Mature faith invites a better understanding. Seekers of truth should not be silenced or shamed. They should be welcomed, encouraged, and respected for wanting to know God more deeply.

It is important to recognize that the dominance of masculine imagery also shaped social expectations. If divine authority is consistently portrayed as male, leadership becomes spiritually coded as masculine. Women may unconsciously internalize the belief that their spiritual role is secondary or supportive to man rather than equal. That subtle conditioning does not always appear overtly oppressive. Sometimes it simply manifests as quiet limitation.

At the same time, men may internalize a narrow definition of strength. If God is always portrayed as stern, commanding, and distant, men may feel pressure to suppress their compassion and tenderness or emotional depth in order to reflect what they believe is divine likeness. Both genders can suffer under imbalance, even when the intention was never to harm.

The image we inherited was not created with malice. It was shaped by history, culture, language, and power structures that existed long before we arrived. Understanding that context allows us to approach this conversation without anger. Expansion does not require condemnation. It requires awareness.

When we pause and really look at the image of God many of us inherited, it becomes clear that much of that picture was shaped by the societies that described it. Words like King, Father, and Lord carried weight in cultures built on hierarchy and authority. Those terms helped people understand power and order in ways that made sense at the time. They were meaningful and useful. They gave structure to something vast and unseen.

At the same time, no single image can fully contain what is infinite. If God is truly everywhere and all powerful, then any one description must be limited. Limited does not mean wrong. It simply means incomplete. A single lens cannot show the whole view. Suggesting that God is expressed only through masculine language quietly raises another question. Does that imply that woman reflects only part of the divine while man reflects the whole? That conclusion does not sit well when we consider that both were created with intelligence, emotion, creativity, and authority.

Recognizing that our understanding may be incomplete is not a rejection of faith. Actually it is a deepening of it. You can still love God and yearn for a deeper, more detailed understanding. Early faith often depends on simple imagery because simplicity is easier to comprehend. As we grow, our capacity expands and we want more. Mature faith can embrace complexity without feeling threatened by it. Expanding our understanding does not weaken belief. It strengthens it by allowing it to breathe.

When we acknowledge that many of our descriptions were shaped by the time in which they were written, we create room for deeper reflection and understanding. What if the divine source contains every quality we have labeled masculine and every quality we have labeled feminine? What if strength and tenderness, structure and intuition, leadership and compassion all flow from the same sacred presence?

To say that God encompasses both is not to speak in biological terms. It is to recognize that what we call masculine and feminine are expressions of energy, character, and function. Both exist within the divine nature, and because we are created in the image of God, both exist within us as well. Each of us carries the capacity for courage and nurture, discipline and empathy, firmness and grace. The balance of these qualities is not divided by anatomy but expressed through the fullness of who we are.

This is not about biology. It is about wholeness. The divine nature is not fragmented, and neither are we. What we often divide into categories of male and female can be understood more deeply as complementary energies that exist within the fullness of God. Created in that image, we too carry both the power to lead and the capacity to nurture, the ability to stand firm and the ability to comfort. Wholeness, not division, reflects the divine.

The purpose of this chapter is not to dismantle tradition. It is to loosen its grip just enough to allow a broader perspective into the conversation. The God many of us were introduced to may have been described through masculine language, but language is a tool, not a cage. Understanding how that image was formed is the first step toward expanding it into something fuller, richer, and more reflective of the divine complexity we seek to know.

2

If God Is Infinite, God Cannot Be Limited

When we describe God as infinite, omnipotent, and omnipresent, those words carry real weight. They are not decorative titles meant to inspire emotion is us. Infinity means without limit. Omnipresence means present everywhere at once. Omnipotence means possessing all power. These are expansive claims without limits. Yet the moment we attach a singular gender to that vastness, we introduce a boundary into something we insist has none. If God is truly without limit, then placing confinement around divine identity deserves thoughtful examination. Limitation and infinity cannot comfortably coexist.

Assigning gender to God feels natural because human beings understand the world through categories and the familiar, repetitive language we have created to make sense of it. We sort, define, and label in order to navigate reality. Male and female are biological distinctions that shape how society functions and how individuals experience life. These categories serve an important purpose within human existence. However, what applies to physical bodies does not automatically apply to divine essence. Gender, as we experience it, belongs to form and biology. God, by definition, transcends both.

To say that God transcends gender does not mean erasing the language of Scripture. It means recognizing the difference between descriptive language and ultimate reality. Words such as Father were used within a cultural framework that understood authority, provision, and leadership through paternal imagery. Those terms communicated relational truth within a historical setting. They were meaningful and effective. At the same time, the reality they point toward must be larger than the metaphor itself.

If the divine source is truly infinite, then every quality we associate with strength, nurturing, structure, compassion, justice, and mercy must originate there. Human beings did not invent these traits out of thin air. We discovered them, expressed them, and named them. They reflect something deeper than culture. When Scripture says both male and female are created in the image of God, that statement deserves careful thought. It suggests that divine fullness cannot be reduced to one side of a human category. Infinity does not divide itself into fragments. It contains the whole.

Saying that male and female reflect God does not mean God is divided into parts. It means that what we see expressed through humanity comes from a unified source. If both were created by God, then both must originate from that same divine intelligence. Just as a child carries genetic material from both parents, humanity carries attributes that originate from the one source that created us. Every person, regardless of gender, reflects aspects of that limitless presence.

Creation cannot contain qualities that do not first exist within its creator. You cannot give what you do not possess. If decisiveness and structure are often labeled masculine, and compassion and intuition are often labeled feminine, then the source that brought both into existence must contain the capacity for both. Otherwise, those qualities would have no origin. They would have appeared from nowhere, and that contradicts the idea of a purposeful Creator.

This perspective changes how we see ourselves. It removes the hierarchy that places one set of traits above another. It allows strength and empathy to coexist without competition. It permits leadership to include tenderness and compassion to include firmness. When we understand that these qualities flow from the same divine source, we stop fragmenting ourselves. We begin integrating.

In practical terms, this understanding empowers growth. A man does not lose masculinity by developing emotional awareness. A woman does not lose femininity by exercising authority. Both are simply expressing dimensions of the divine image already present within them. The imbalance happens when we suppress half of what we were designed to embody.

Recognizing this wholeness also deepens responsibility. If divine qualities live within us, then how we express them matters. Strength should not become domination. Compassion should not become weakness. Structure should not harden into control. Intuition should not drift into avoidance. Balance becomes essential because we are reflecting something sacred.

When you begin to see yourself as carrying both power and tenderness, clarity and empathy, courage and care, your sense of identity expands. You are not limited to narrow definitions shaped by culture. You are a reflection of something infinite. That realization should not inflate ego. It should elevate purpose. You were created to express the fullness of the source that created you, not just a fraction of it.

Genesis offers a profound line that many read but do not pause to examine closely. Humanity was created in the image of God, male and female. That verse does not separate divine likeness into two unrelated parts. It presents both expressions together under one image. If we accept that statement at face value, then divine image includes duality.

Some argue that calling God Father is simply relational language used for connection. That explanation makes sense within its historical context. In ancient cultures, fatherhood represented provision and protection. The metaphor communicated authority and care. The issue arises only when metaphor becomes exclusion. When Father language is interpreted as biological maleness rather than relational symbolism, infinity is unintentionally reduced.

Consider something practical. If someone describes the ocean as powerful, we understand that power is a characteristic, not a gender. If someone describes light as strong, we do not imagine it as male. When we describe divine qualities such as mercy, justice, love, or strength, those characteristics are not inherently gendered. They are human interpretations layered onto energetic expressions.

Divine source is not anatomical. It is not limited by chromosomes or reproductive function. The presence that sustains galaxies and regulates cellular healing is not confined to male biology. Gender belongs to embodiment. Divinity belongs to essence.

The tension many people feel when hearing the phrase "God is not a man" often comes from fear that removing masculinity removes authority. In some traditions, masculinity has been equated with order, protection, and leadership. Yet those qualities do not disappear when we expand our understanding of God. They simply cease to be gender exclusive.

Authority does not require maleness. Compassion does not require femaleness. Both are expressions of intelligent power. When we detach divine characteristics from gender labels, something remarkable happens. We begin to see balance instead of hierarchy.

An infinite being cannot be less than what it creates. Humanity expresses a wide spectrum of personality, emotion, logic, creativity, softness, and strength. If God is the source of humanity, then divine nature must be capable of expressing the fullness of that spectrum.

Restricting that fullness to one side of the human experience diminishes the very omnipotence we claim to honor.

Some will insist that scripture consistently refers to God using masculine pronouns. That is true in many translations. It is also true that ancient languages were structured differently than modern English. Hebrew, for example, assigns gender to nouns in ways that do not always translate cleanly. The word for spirit in Hebrew, "ruach," carries feminine grammatical form. In Greek, the word "pneuma" is neuter. Linguistic nuance complicates simplistic conclusions.

Understanding that context does not erase faith. It enriches it. It allows believers to see how language shaped theology without reducing theology to language.

At the heart of this conversation is not rebellion but coherence. If we proclaim that God is all, then we must allow that statement to remain logically consistent. All cannot mean male alone. All cannot exclude half of humanity. All must include.

Expanding our understanding of divine nature does not strip away reverence. It invites awe. A God confined to one gender feels smaller. A God who contains the fullness of both masculine and feminine expressions feels worthy of the word infinite.

When infinity is honored fully, limitation falls away naturally.

In59Seconds Publishing Co

3

Ancient Wisdom, Not Modern Ideas

There is something almost amusing about hearing certain spiritual concepts labeled as modern, as if humanity just discovered the power of thought or the importance of meditation in the last few decades. The truth is that these ideas have been circulating for centuries. They have simply been renamed, repackaged, and rediscovered by each new generation that believes it has found something revolutionary.

I collect vintage books from the eighteen hundreds and early nineteen hundreds that speak boldly about imagination shaping experience, about belief influencing circumstance, about divine law responding to mental focus. Writers from those eras discussed what many now call manifestation. They wrote about the kingdom within, about thought as creative force, about aligning oneself with higher intelligence. Long before social media coined new phrases, people were already exploring these principles deeply.

Meditation was not invented by wellness influencers. Positive thinking was not born in motivational seminars. Sound healing, sacred geometry, breath work, inner kingdom consciousness, these were practiced, studied, and honored across civilizations. What changes is not truth itself, but the language used to describe it.

During my own search for God and for a fuller understanding of divine presence, I realized that limiting spiritual conversation to one tradition often blinds us to the vastness of what humanity has already explored. I grew up in the Church of God in Christ. My grandmother raised me in that faith. I am grateful for it. In some of the darkest seasons of my life, the church grounded me. It gave me structure when I needed it. It gave me community when I felt alone. I do not speak against it. I honor it.

At the same time, something in me knew there was more to understand.

Curiosity is not rebellion. It is hunger.

That hunger led me beyond familiar walls. It led me into history, into other cultures, into sacred spaces that existed long before modern denominations were formed. It forced me to confront how small my mental box had been.

Ancient civilizations did not all worship the same way, yet each honored something greater than themselves. Egyptians spoke of cosmic order and divine balance. Greeks sought wisdom through philosophy and sacred ritual. Indigenous traditions aligned with the elements of earth, air, fire, and water. Monasteries in remote mountains held silence as sacred discipline. The language differed. The clothing differed. The rituals differed. The reverence did not.

Standing inside ancient structures, reading texts that predate modern theology, and studying spiritual systems across time made one thing undeniable. Humanity has always sensed that there is a governing intelligence behind existence. Humanity has always wrestled with how to describe it. Humanity has always expressed it through the lens of culture.

When we label these explorations as new age or modern, we overlook the depth of history behind them. We forget that entire civilizations organized their lives around divine law long before our current religious frameworks existed. We assume ownership of truth instead of recognizing participation in it.

What became clear to me is that the principles themselves are universal. You reap what you sow. What you focus on grows. Belief shapes experience. Energy follows attention. Actions produce consequence. These are not trendy affirmations. They are patterns embedded into existence.

Gravity does not care what religion you practice. If you jump from a building, you will fall. Universal law functions the same way. Kindness produces a different atmosphere than cruelty. Love yields different outcomes than bitterness. Integrity stabilizes life. Deception destabilizes it. These principles operate whether acknowledged or not.

Understanding that humbled me.

It stripped away arrogance. It dissolved the need to argue whose label for God was correct. The deeper realization was that divine intelligence responds to belief and alignment more than to terminology. It truly is done unto you as you believe.

When you see that truth echoed across cultures and centuries, it becomes difficult to cling tightly to the idea that one expression holds exclusive ownership of God. It becomes easier to recognize that humanity has been circling the same mystery in different languages for thousands of years.

This recognition did not weaken my faith. It deepened it. It made me more respectful of others. It made me less defensive. It made me less inclined to judge how someone else prays, kneels, chants, or meditates.

The search for God has never belonged to one era or one denomination. It belongs to humanity.

And that realization was only the beginning of my journey.

In59SecondsPublishing Co

4

The Balance Within Creation

When we step back and observe the natural world without inherited assumptions guiding our interpretation, something becomes unmistakably clear. Life does not function through isolation. It does not move forward through singular dominance. Creation advances through balance. Complementary forces work together in structured harmony, and from that cooperation, life continues.

A farmer understands this without needing a theological debate. Crops do not reproduce in isolation. Pollination requires transfer. In flowering plants, male reproductive structures produce pollen while female structures receive it. Fertilization depends on interaction. Even in plants that contain both reproductive components within a single organism, reproduction still requires the exchange of material. Growth depends on balance. Harvest depends on complement.

The animal kingdom reflects the same principle. Most species require both male and female participation in order to reproduce. Fertilization depends on two distinct biological contributions. The female body nurtures and carries life. The male body contributes genetic material necessary for conception. Remove either contribution and reproduction stops. Life advances through partnership.

Human beings are no exception. Every child carries twenty three chromosomes from the mother and twenty three from the father. That blending forms a completely new genetic identity. Neither parent alone can generate a full human being. Biology itself insists on balance. Life cannot come forth without the female. Not one of us would be here if women did not exist. This is not ideology. It is observable, irrefutable reality.

The pattern does not stop with biology. It shows up in physics and in the way energy moves through the material world. Electricity works because of polarity. A battery has a positive end and a negative end. Power flows because those two opposites connect. If you remove one side, nothing works. Energy moves when opposites meet and interact.

Even Nikola Tesla understood this. He studied how energy transfers and how opposing forces create motion and power. The principle is actually quite simple. For energy to flow, there must be balance between two complementary sides. Creation reflects this everywhere. What we call male and female in the physical world mirrors a deeper energetic reality. Life and power move forward through balance, not through one side alone.

Magnets operate the same exact way. North and south poles create magnetic fields through relationship. Even if you break a magnet in half, each fragment still forms both poles. Polarity is built into the structure itself.

In physics, motion depends on interaction between forces. When one force pushes, another responds. Pressure meets resistance. Stability forms when opposing influences balance each other instead of overpowering one another. The universe does not operate through a single force acting alone. It operates through relationship.

Look at something as simple as walking. Every step requires balance between gravity pulling you downward and muscles pushing upward. Without gravity, you would float without control. Without muscular resistance, you would collapse. Movement happens because two forces work together in tension. That tension is not conflict. It is cooperation.

The same principle shows up in sound waves. Vibration travels because of alternating patterns of compression and expansion. Air molecules move back and forth, creating rhythm. Without that exchange, there would be silence. Light behaves in dual ways as well, functioning as both particle and wave. Scientists refer to this as wave particle duality. Reality itself contains paired behavior working together in order to function.

When we step back and notice how often this pattern appears, it becomes difficult to ignore. Movement, sound, light, breath, and biological life all operate through complementary interaction. That consistent pairing across creation reflects something deeper than coincidence. It mirrors the balance of male and female cooperation that makes human life possible. If dual participation is woven into the fabric of physics and biology, then reducing the divine source to one gender alone contradicts the very structure embedded in the universe. The design itself suggests fullness, not singular limitation.

Day and night form another example. The earth rotates, creating alternating cycles of light and darkness, and plants depend on both. Too much sunlight scorches them. Constant darkness prevents growth. Balance allows them to thrive.

I remember when I tried to grow cantaloupe in my home garden. The vines were healthy, the leaves were strong, but the fruit just was not coming in the way I expected. I stood there looking at those plants wondering what I was doing wrong. A friend of mine laughed gently and explained that I needed to manually pollinate them. He showed me how to take pollen from the male flower and transfer it to the female bloom. At first it felt a little awkward, almost scientific for something happening in my backyard, but once I understood the difference between the male and female flowers, it suddenly made sense.

After I started cross pollinating them correctly, everything changed.

The next harvest was abundant. What had once felt confusing became simple. What once felt unproductive became fruitful. That little garden lesson stayed with me because it was such a clear picture of how life works. The fruit did not come from the male flower alone. It did not come from the female flower alone. It came from the cooperation of both.

The same rhythm shows up everywhere. Inhaling and exhaling sustain breath. The heart contracts and then relaxes to pump blood effectively. Muscles tighten and release to create movement. Even productivity requires rest to remain sustainable. Life flourishes through the rhythm between complementary forces working together.

And when you begin to see that rhythm woven into everything, it becomes harder to accept the idea that the source of all creation could exist as only one side of that design.

The same rhythm shows up everywhere. Inhaling and exhaling sustain breath. The heart contracts and then relaxes to pump blood effectively. Muscles tighten and release to create movement. Even productivity requires rest in order to remain sustainable. Life flourishes through the rhythm between complementary forces working together.

When you begin to recognize that pattern woven into gardens, bodies, ecosystems, and energy itself, it becomes difficult to believe that the source behind all of it exists as only one side of the design. Creation consistently reflects balance. The origin of creation must reflect it as well.

The universe functions through structured duality. Opposing forces are not enemies. They are partners in maintaining balance. When this pattern appears consistently across physics, biology, and daily life, it becomes difficult to ignore. Complement is not accidental. It is built into the framework of existence.

Agriculture depends on understanding this balance. Farmers selectively breed livestock by pairing male and female animals with desirable traits. Genetic diversity strengthens herds. Crops are cross pollinated to enhance resilience. Knowledge of male and female reproductive systems within plants allows harvest to continue season after season.

Ecosystems reflect interdependence. Bees rely on nectar for survival. Flowers rely on bees for pollination. Predator and prey populations regulate one another to maintain ecological stability. Remove one part of the system and imbalance spreads quickly. Creation consistently demonstrates cooperation between complementary elements.

If the source of all creation established this pattern, then that source must contain the capacity from which both complementary aspects originate. It would be illogical to assume that the designer of balance exists in imbalance. It would be inconsistent to claim that the architect of dual participation embodies only one side of the design.

When many people hear masculine language used for God, they assume literal male identity. Yet masculinity as humans experience it belongs to biology. It involves chromosomes, hormones, anatomy, and reproductive function. Spirit does not possess chromosomes. Infinity does not require anatomy. If divine source transcends physical form, then gender as a biological category cannot define it.

Language was shaped within historical cultures. In ancient societies, authority was associated primarily with fathers. Leadership, inheritance, and protection were often concentrated within patriarchal structures. Referring to God as Father communicated sovereignty and relational closeness in a way people understood at that time. The metaphor was effective. It conveyed strength, provision, and covenant. Metaphor, however, is not limitation.

Reducing divine essence to male biology because masculine pronouns were used in Scripture narrows what Scripture itself presents as infinite. When Genesis states that both male and female were created in the image of God, the implication is profound. The image is reflected in both. The source must therefore be larger than either category alone.

Creation cannot contain qualities that do not first exist within its creator. You cannot give what you do not possess. If strength, decisiveness, and structural leadership are often labeled masculine, and compassion, nurture, and intuitive sensitivity are often labeled feminine, then the source from which both arise must contain the capacity for both. Otherwise those qualities would emerge from nowhere.

Human beings frequently divide these traits into gendered categories, yet lived experience proves that both exist within individuals regardless of sex. A father can nurture with tenderness. A mother can lead with authority. Both can protect fiercely. Both can discipline wisely. These qualities are not owned exclusively by one gender. They are expressions of deeper energetic patterns.

The design of reproduction underscores the importance of the feminine contribution. A fertilized egg does not grow in the male body. It develops within the female body. The womb nourishes, protects, and sustains life for months before birth. Without that environment, human existence would not continue. This reality carries theological weight.

If life requires both male and female participation, then the source of life cannot be meaningfully described as male alone. A male body does not generate life independently. Creation demands complement. Divine source must be whole enough to originate both.

Some species reproduce asexually under certain conditions. Certain fish and reptiles have demonstrated parthenogenesis, where females produce offspring without male fertilization. Yet even in those cases, the species evolved from male and female systems. The biological blueprint still reflects differentiation. The exception does not erase the foundational design.

Energy systems reinforce the same lesson.

- Electrical current requires positive and negative polarity.
- Magnetic fields require north and south orientation.

- Chemical reactions depend on interaction between distinct elements.
- Day and night cycles regulate ecological rhythms.
- Inhalation and exhalation sustain respiration.

Balance produces continuity.

When discussing divine nature, acknowledging this pattern restores dignity to the feminine without diminishing the masculine. It affirms that nurture is not weakness. It confirms that compassion is not secondary to strength. It recognizes that receptivity and intuition are not inferior qualities but essential ones.

Viewing God as exclusively male can subtly distort self perception. If divinity is male and male alone, women may feel spiritually derivative rather than equally reflective of divine image. That conclusion contradicts the foundational claim that both male and female bear that image fully. The balance within creation suggests something more expansive. The source of life must be complete.

Completeness does not imply confusion. It does not erase distinction, It encompasses it. Male and female exist as differentiated expressions within creation. The source from which they arise must contain the fullness that allows both to emerge.

Understanding this reshapes identity. Men do not lose strength by developing emotional depth. Women do not lose femininity by exercising authority. Both are expressing dimensions of a complete image. Imbalance occurs when one side is exaggerated and the other suppressed.

Cultural conditioning has often elevated masculine coded traits such as dominance, control, and decisiveness while undervaluing empathy, receptivity, and relational sensitivity. Creation itself contradicts that imbalance. No human being enters the world without passing through the body of a woman. Life begins in nurture.

Agriculture again provides clarity. Seeds require soil. Soil provides environment. Without receptive ground, seed remains potential rather than reality. Contribution and reception work together.

Electricity once more offers illustration. A battery does not produce usable energy from a single terminal. The positive and negative poles exist in relationship. Energy flows because of difference held in balance. Creation repeatedly teaches the same lesson. Complement produces continuity.

If divine source established this structure, then divine source must embody fullness rather than singular limitation.

This understanding does not dismantle faith. It deepens it. It invites mature reflection rather than blind acceptance. It encourages alignment between theology and observable reality.

The balance within creation points toward a source that is not fragmented. Masculine language in Scripture communicates authority and relational intimacy. Maternal metaphors within Scripture communicate nurture and compassion. Both point toward the same divine essence.

Infinity has no need for chromosomes. Spirit has no need for anatomy.God is not confined to male biology. God is the source from which male and female both originate.

When that truth settles deeply, spiritual identity stabilizes. Women no longer need to justify their spiritual authority. Men no longer need to suppress gentleness to appear aligned with divine image. Both stand equally reflective of the source that created them. Creation teaches balance.

The soil and seed teach it. The chromosome and fertilization teach it. The battery and magnetic field teach it. The ecosystem and agricultural cycle teach it. The balance within creation reflects the fullness of its source.

Recognizing this does not threaten tradition. It honors design. It respects biology. It acknowledges energy systems. It affirms spiritual wholeness. Divine source is not reduced to manhood it is the origin of both man and woman, and life continues because balance remains embedded in the architecture of existence.

5

The Search That Opened My Mind

There came a point in my life when reading was no longer enough. Studying theology from a distance could only take me so far. I wanted to stand where ancient people stood. I wanted to feel what they felt. I wanted to see how other cultures honored the divine with my own eyes instead of filtering everything through the lens I had inherited.

That desire led me to Egypt.

Walking through Cairo, traveling to Aswan, standing in Hurghada, I could feel history pressing against the present. The Giza pyramids are not just monuments. They are reminders that entire civilizations organized their existence around sacred understanding. When I went inside the Great Pyramid and sat in the King's Chamber, I did not feel rebellion against my faith. I felt reverence. I meditated there, not out of defiance, but out of curiosity and humility. I carried personal crystals into the Temple of Isis and placed them gently on the altar, not because I had abandoned what I believed, but because I wanted to experience how other cultures expressed devotion.

Standing before the statue of Sekhmet, I felt the weight of symbolism and power that predates modern denominations. Ancient Egypt understood balance between masculine and feminine energies long before those words became trendy in Western conversation. Divine expressions were not confined to a single gender. Strength and fertility, destruction and creation, protection and nurture, all were acknowledged within their spiritual system. From Egypt, my journey continued across continents.

In Indonesia, I entered sacred temples and prayed at water fountains considered holy by the people who gathered there. The rituals were different, they honored God with beautiful flower arrangements. The language was also different. The gestures were different, they would all drop at the sound of a bell and bow to God throughout the day. Yet the sincerity in the faces of those praying looked exactly the same as the sincerity I had seen in church pews growing up. Watching people honor God in ways unfamiliar to me expanded something inside my heart. It forced me to confront how small my previous box had been.

Machu Picchu brought another layer of awareness. Standing on those ancient stones, high above the clouds, surrounded by the remains of a civilization that once ordered its life around cosmic alignment, I felt humility. I walked through sacred buildings, meditated on mountain-tops, and participated in ceremonies honoring fire, air, earth, and water with a private shaman in Cusco, Peru. The experience was not about abandoning Jesus or replacing my faith. It was about understanding that humanity has always sought connection with something greater.

Greece offered yet another dimension. In Meteora and Delphi, monasteries carved into cliffs held centuries of prayer within their walls. Silence there felt alive. Devotion there felt disciplined and focused. Even in traditions structured differently than my own upbringing, the hunger for divine connection remained consistent.

For a season, I joined the Theosophy Society and attended book studies, listening carefully to how they interpreted universal law and divine consciousness. I spent time within conscious communities, listening to drums, learning about Kemet, studying the laws of Ma'at and the principle of balance. Each environment added perspective. Each one stretched my understanding.

Some might hear all of that and assume confusion. What I found was clarity.

Traveling across continents did not fracture my belief in God. It purified it. It stripped away arrogance. It humbled me deeply. When you see people in Egypt, Indonesia, Peru, and Greece all honoring divine presence with sincerity, it becomes impossible to believe that only one cultural expression has a monopoly on truth. It becomes clear that it is truly done unto you as you believe.

That realization softens judgment. It reduces the urge to argue over whose path is correct. It teaches respect. Every country honors God differently. Every culture interprets divine presence through its own history and symbolism. The deeper commonality is not ritual. It is reverence.

My upbringing in the Church of God in Christ still matters to me. It saved my life during seasons when I needed structure and spiritual grounding. I still believe in the divine source. I still believe in higher power. I still believe in Jesus Christ. My travels did not erase that. They refined it.

I have come to believe that Jesus did not perform miracles to intimidate humanity, but to reveal potential. His message, as I understand it now, was not meant to impress us into smallness. It was meant to awaken us into participation. The same creative intelligence that animated his life animates ours. The difference is awareness.

In the end, after pyramids and monasteries, temples and ceremonies, societies and studies, I arrived at something profoundly simple. There is an amazing divine source governing existence. Universal laws operate whether we acknowledge them or not. Just as gravity ensures that a body falls when it leaps from a building, spiritual law ensures that actions carry consequence. Kindness produces one result. Bitterness produces another. Love multiplies differently than hatred.

The simplicity of that truth brought peace.

Search is not blasphemy. Questioning is not disrespect. Stepping outside a narrow frame to explore does not offend God. It honors the mind and curiosity that divine intelligence placed within us.

What matters is not which country you traveled to, which ceremony you attended, or which name you used in prayer. What matters is alignment. Show love if you want love returned. Practice kindness if you desire kindness. Honor God in a way that uplifts you and allows others the dignity of honoring God in the way that uplifts them.

My journey came full circle. I did not abandon faith. I expanded it. I no longer feel compelled to declare that one denomination holds exclusive access to divine truth. Each person has the right to choose their path. Respecting that does not weaken belief. It strengthens humility.

Standing in ancient temples and modern churches, on mountaintops and inside pyramids, in sacred silence and rhythmic drums, one truth remained steady. Divine presence is larger than any single box we attempt to contain it in.

And when you realize that, you stop arguing.

You start respecting. You start living.

#In59Seconds

6

The Divine Masculine and the Divine Feminine Explained

When people hear the terms divine masculine and divine feminine, confusion often follows. Some assume it is about gender roles. Others assume it is about biological identity. Some dismiss it entirely because the language sounds unfamiliar or modern. In reality, this conversation is not about biology. It is about energy, expression, and balance.

Masculine and feminine energies are not labels for men and women. They are descriptions of qualities that exist within every human being. These qualities shape how we lead, nurture, create, protect, decide, and relate. They are not competitive forces. They are complementary ones.

Masculine energy, in its healthy form, expresses structure and direction. It brings order to chaos. It builds frameworks. It sets boundaries. It initiates movement. There is strength in it, decisiveness in it, protection in it. Healthy masculine energy is steady. It is reliable. It is focused. It provides containment so that growth can happen safely.

Feminine energy, in its healthy form, expresses intuition and creativity. It nurtures what has been built. It receives. It feels deeply. It adapts. There is softness in it, but that softness is not weakness. It carries emotional intelligence, insight, and the ability to perceive nuance. Healthy feminine energy flows. It inspires. It connects.

Both energies are necessary. Without structure, creativity becomes scattered. Without creativity, structure becomes rigid. Without boundaries, love can become chaotic. Without love, boundaries become harsh. Balance is what makes power sustainable.

As a business owner managing a large salon with multiple employees, I experienced this balance firsthand. There were seasons when I had to operate strongly in masculine energy. Decisions had to be made. Standards had to be enforced. Authority had to be clear. Running a business requires structure. It requires firmness. It requires direction.

At the same time, leadership cannot survive on authority alone. Returning to softness was essential. Listening to staff concerns. Offering grace. Understanding emotional dynamics. Encouraging growth rather than simply enforcing rules. That required feminine energy. Without it, the environment would have become cold and transactional.

The mistake many people make is assuming that expressing masculine energy makes a woman less feminine, or that expressing feminine energy makes a man less strong. In reality, imbalance creates distortion, not the presence of either energy.

When masculine energy becomes excessive and disconnected from compassion, it can turn controlling, aggressive, or domineering. When feminine energy becomes excessive and disconnected from structure, it can turn passive, indecisive, or overly dependent. Neither extreme reflects divine balance.

Cultural conditioning has often praised men for dominance while discouraging emotional expression. Women have often been praised for gentleness while discouraged from authority. These expectations can cause internal conflict. A woman who feels decisive may question herself. A man who feels deeply may suppress his sensitivity. The result is fragmentation.

Divine balance offers integration instead of suppression.

If God contains both the qualities we describe as masculine and feminine, then expressing both does not move us away from divine image. It moves us closer to it. Authority and compassion can coexist. Strength and tenderness can coexist. Logic and intuition can coexist. These are not contradictions. They are complements.

Understanding this changes how we see ourselves and others. A woman operating in strong leadership is not betraying femininity. A man expressing emotional depth is not betraying masculinity. They are simply drawing from the full spectrum available to them.

Balance requires awareness. It requires the willingness to ask whether we are leaning too heavily into one expression at the expense of the other. It requires humility to adjust when needed. Sometimes we need firmness. Sometimes we need grace. Wisdom lies in knowing which moment requires which energy.

When people label someone as too masculine or too feminine, what they are often sensing is imbalance, not identity. That distinction matters. Imbalance can be corrected. Identity does not need correction.

Recognizing that we all carry both energies creates compassion. It reduces judgment. It allows individuals to stop apologizing for qualities that are part of their divine design. It invites wholeness.

Divine source is not half. It is whole. If we are made in that image, then wholeness is available to us as well.

Understanding masculine and feminine energy is not about redefining gender. It is about restoring balance, and balance is where peace lives.

#In59Seconds

7

When Energy Is Out of Balance

Balance is not automatic. It requires awareness. Most of us were not taught how to recognize imbalance within ourselves because we were busy trying to meet cultural expectations instead of examining internal harmony. When masculine and feminine energies are misunderstood, they often become distorted.

Healthy masculine energy builds and protects. Unhealthy masculine energy controls and dominates. When structure loses compassion, it turns rigid. When decisiveness loses humility, it becomes arrogance. When authority loses empathy, it becomes oppression. None of those distortions reflect divine strength. They reflect imbalance.

Healthy feminine energy nurtures and inspires. Unhealthy feminine energy can become overly passive, overly dependent, or emotionally manipulative when disconnected from grounded strength. When compassion loses boundaries, it turns into self neglect. When receptivity loses discernment, it becomes vulnerability without protection. That is not divine softness. That is imbalance.

Society has often rewarded men for leaning excessively into dominance while discouraging emotional depth. At the same time, women have been encouraged toward agreeableness while quietly criticized for authority. Those pressures create internal conflict. Men may suppress their intuition because it feels too gentle. Women may suppress their assertiveness because it feels too strong. Both lose parts of themselves in the process.

Imbalance rarely announces itself loudly. It shows up in subtle ways. A leader who cannot admit mistakes. A partner who cannot express vulnerability. A parent who disciplines without warmth. A caregiver who gives until they are depleted. These patterns do not mean someone is broken. They mean something within them is leaning too heavily in one direction.

When divine balance is understood, the goal shifts from performance to integration. Instead of asking whether a quality makes you more masculine or more feminine, the question becomes whether that quality is aligned and healthy. Strength anchored in love looks very different from strength anchored in ego. Softness grounded in wisdom looks very different from softness rooted in fear.

Many people who feel judged as too feminine or too masculine are simply expressing a dominant energy without realizing they have access to its complement. A woman who leads decisively may need to consciously reconnect with rest and receptivity. A man who prides himself on emotional control may need to reconnect with tenderness and openness. Neither adjustment diminishes identity. It restores balance.

Divine source contains both energies without conflict. Nature demonstrates this constantly. The earth is both fertile and firm. Water is both gentle and powerful. Fire both destroys and purifies. These forces are not contradictory. They are dynamic. When they remain within balance, life flourishes. When they move to extremes, destruction follows.

Internal imbalance eventually manifests externally. Relationships strain. Work environments become tense. Spiritual practice feels dry or chaotic. Restoring balance requires self reflection rather than blame. It asks where structure needs softness and where softness needs structure.

Awareness is not shame. Recognizing imbalance does not mean condemning yourself. It simply means noticing where you have leaned too far in one direction. Correction can be gentle. Growth can be intentional.

When balance is restored, something settles. Confidence feels steady rather than forceful. Compassion feels strong rather than fragile. Decisions feel clear rather than reactive. You stop performing strength. You embody it. You stop performing gentleness. You live it.

Divine harmony is not about eliminating one energy. It is about honoring both, and when both are honored, you feel whole.

GOD IS NOT A MAN
#In59Seconds

8

The Divine Nature Beyond Gender

Throughout Scripture, God is overwhelmingly referred to using masculine pronouns and titles. Words such as Father, Lord, and King appear repeatedly in both Old and New Testament texts. For many readers, this language shapes their earliest understanding of the divine. It influences how God is imagined, how prayer is formed, and how authority is conceptualized. Yet careful study of Scripture reveals that while masculine language is consistently used, the nature of God cannot be confined to biological categories.

To understand this properly, we must separate grammatical form from metaphysical essence.

The Language of Scripture and Masculine Grammar

The Hebrew Scriptures primarily refer to God using grammatically masculine forms. The name Elohim appears in Genesis 1:1, describing God as Creator of the heavens and the earth. Though the term itself is grammatically plural, it functions with singular verbs, emphasizing divine unity. The covenant name YHWH, often rendered as Yahweh in English transliteration, also carries masculine grammatical markers in

Hebrew usage.

When the Hebrew Bible was translated into Greek through the Septuagint centuries before Christ, masculine pronouns continued to be used. The New Testament, written in Koine Greek, follows the same pattern. Jesus teaches His followers to pray, "Our Father in heaven," reinforcing relational language grounded in paternal imagery.

Historical manuscript evidence supports this consistency. The Dead Sea Scrolls, which contain some of the earliest surviving Old Testament texts, preserve masculine references in alignment with later Masoretic manuscripts. Early Greek codices of the New Testament reflect the same grammatical structure. Across centuries of transmission, the masculine form remains stable.

Yet grammar does not equal biology.

Hebrew and Greek nouns are assigned grammatical gender. This does not imply physical form. The masculine grammatical structure tells us how language functioned in ancient cultures. It does not suggest that God possesses a male body.

Fatherhood as Relational Language

The title "Father" holds profound theological meaning. In ancient Near Eastern culture, fatherhood implied responsibility, protection, provision, inheritance, and covenant leadership. To call God "Father" was not merely to identify Him with maleness. It was to describe His relational authority.

Scriptural passages frequently emphasize paternal compassion. Psalm 103 compares divine mercy to a father's compassion toward his children. Deuteronomy presents God as Creator and covenant parent who formed and sustained Israel. In the New Testament, believers are described as adopted children, receiving the Spirit of adoption through which they cry out in intimacy and trust.

The father metaphor communicates relational closeness combined with moral authority. It portrays God as both a sovereign ruler and a personal protector. The emphasis or focus is not on anatomy or physical form, but on responsibility, commitment and the responsibility to guide, provide, and remain faithful.

Maternal Imagery Within Scripture

While masculine pronouns dominate biblical language, Scripture does not restrict divine imagery exclusively to paternal metaphors. Several passages employ maternal analogies to illustrate God's nurturing and protective character.

Isaiah compares divine comfort to that of a mother consoling her child. Hosea describes God's protective intensity using imagery associated with maternal ferocity. Elsewhere, prophetic literature depicts God's care in terms reminiscent of labor, birth, and nursing.

These passages do not alter the grammatical norm, yet they expand the conceptual understanding of divine character. Compassion, nurture, and tenderness are not presented as exclusively feminine traits but as attributes inherent in God's nature.

The inclusion of maternal imagery demonstrates that Scripture is comfortable drawing from the full range of human relational experience to describe divine activity.

God as Spirit

One of the clearest theological statements about God's nature appears in the Gospel of John. Jesus declares that God is Spirit and must be worshiped in spirit and truth. This statement moves the discussion beyond gendered language entirely.

Spirit, by definition, transcends physical form. Biological categories belong to embodied creatures. God, as Creator, is not bound by human limitations. The divine nature cannot be reduced to male or female because those distinctions arise within creation itself.

Genesis affirms that humanity is created in the image of God, both male and female. This dual reflection suggests that divine likeness is expressed across the full spectrum of human embodiment. Neither man nor woman alone exhausts the image. Together they reflect aspects of divine creativity and relational capacity.

The implication is profound. God is not male in a biological sense, nor female. Divine essence surpasses the categories assigned to created beings.

Manuscript Continuity and Historical Transmission

Early Jewish and Christian communities preserved Scripture with remarkable care. Manuscript traditions such as the Dead Sea Scrolls and early Greek New Testament codices demonstrate consistent use of masculine pronouns across centuries.

This continuity indicates intentional preservation rather than accidental drift. Biblical authors deliberately employed paternal language to communicate theological truth within their cultural framework.

At the same time, the consistency of language does not imply exclusivity of essence. Ancient authors used the linguistic tools available to them. Masculine grammatical form functioned as the standard for authority titles in those societies. The historical context explains the form without confining the nature.

Theological Significance of Fatherhood

Calling God "Father" carries covenant implications. It signals origin, inheritance, discipline, and belonging. In Ephesians, God is described as Father over all, through all, and in all. Romans speaks of adoption into divine family.

Fatherhood establishes relational intimacy while maintaining sovereignty. It bridges transcendence and nearness. The metaphor conveys trust and authority simultaneously.

Yet theology consistently affirms that metaphors serve understanding. They are descriptive tools, not literal anatomical claims.

Metaphor and Divine Mystery

Scripture uses many human images to describe God. King, Shepherd, Warrior, Judge, Rock, Refuge. Each metaphor reveals something true while leaving other aspects unexplained.

No single image captures divine fullness. Even Solomon acknowledges that the heavens cannot contain God. Human language stretches toward mystery but never fully encloses it.

Masculine pronouns function within that broader symbolic framework. They communicate relationship, order, covenant, and authority. They do not define divine biology.

Understanding this distinction prevents unnecessary tension. One can affirm the traditional language of Scripture while recognizing that God's essence transcends physical categories.

Gender and the Image of God

Genesis presents humanity as created in divine image, both male and female. This statement has sparked extensive theological reflection. If both sexes reflect divine likeness, then divine nature must be broad enough to encompass attributes associated with each.

Qualities culturally labeled masculine or feminine ultimately originate in God. Strength and compassion, justice and mercy, structure and nurture all find their source in the divine.

This does not dissolve biblical language. In the contrary It deepens it. The father metaphor remains meaningful while acknowledging that God's being cannot be confined to a single human category.

Faith Maturing Through Understanding

For many believers, questioning gender language can feel destabilizing. Yet deeper study often strengthens faith rather than weakens it. Recognizing that metaphors function as bridges rather than boundaries allows belief to mature.

Faith need not cling rigidly to imagery in order to remain faithful. It can honor tradition while understanding historical context. It can appreciate paternal language while affirming divine transcendence.

This maturation does not dismantle Scripture. It refines interpretation.

Conclusion: Language as Tool, Not Limitation

The Bible consistently refers to God using masculine pronouns and titles. Historical manuscripts confirm that this usage was deliberate and sustained. Fatherhood imagery conveys authority, protection, covenant, and intimacy in ways ancient audiences understood clearly.

At the same time, Scripture affirms that God is Spirit, beyond flesh and biological limitation. Maternal analogies appear when divine nurture must be emphasized. Humanity, both male and female, bears the image of God, pointing toward a nature that transcends gendered categories.

Language serves as a tool to communicate divine truth. It guides understanding without confining essence. Recognizing this distinction allows believers to approach Scripture with reverence and depth, honoring tradition while acknowledging the fullness of divine mystery.

God's nature is not reduced by metaphor. It is revealed through it, even as it remains greater than any single word can contain.

9

Divine Source in Motion

Many people hear the word energy and immediately think of physical stamina. How fast can you get up in the morning. How productive are you. How long can you push through the day. That is one form of energy, but it is only the surface.

This chapter speaks of something deeper. The invisible yet powerful frequency that shapes existence itself. Everything is energy. And if everything is energy, then God, the Source of all things, must be understood as the highest, most intelligent form of that energy.

If God is infinite, then God cannot be limited to a gender. Gender belongs to biology. Energy belongs to eternity.

When I say everything is energy, I mean everything. The chair you sit in. The desk at work. The rock outside. The trees lining the street. The tomatoes growing in a garden. Even your thoughts. Your unseen thoughts are energy. They are vibrating particles in motion, shaping perception and experience.

Science calls it matter in motion. Spirituality calls it life force.

Scripture calls it breath. Different languages. Same truth.

Once I understood this, my perception shifted. Flowers were no longer just decorations. Trees were no longer background scenery. They carried vibration, intelligence, and rhythm. Their stillness was alive. Their beauty felt intentional. I began noticing trees I had passed for decades without seeing. When I traveled to New Mexico and witnessed the fall foliage, I felt awe, not just for color, but for frequency. Creation hums.

Now it may be easier to accept that living things carry energy, but it can be more difficult to imagine that inanimate objects are also energy. Yet physics confirms that everything is composed of vibrating particles. The difference between a tree and a table is vibrational density, not substance.

Everything is made of the same divine substance, vibrating at different speeds.

If that is true, then God is not an elderly man seated somewhere beyond the clouds. God is the eternal field of intelligence from which all vibration flows. God is not male. God is Source.

And within that Source, masculine and feminine energies are expressions, not divisions.

The Language of Energy

Webster defines energy as the capacity to perform work. Physics describes it as kinetic, potential, thermal, chemical, and electromagnetic. These definitions may sound technical, but beneath the terminology lies a simple truth. Energy is the ability to cause change.

When you wake up excited about the day, that excitement is energy. When anger rises in your body and your voice follows, that is energy. When you hand a cashier money, you are transferring energy.

Energy is neutral until directed.

Spiritually, energy is described as life force. Chi. Prana. Holy Spirit. Breath. It is the unseen current connecting everything. Whether someone calls it God, Universe, Yahweh, or simply divine intelligence, the concept remains steady. There is an intelligent force animating existence.

If God is the Source of all life force, then God cannot be reduced to a masculine personality. Energy itself is not male or female. It expresses through both.

Forms of Energy, Expressions of the Divine

Thermal energy warms your skin in sunlight. It keeps your body alive. Science teaches that energy cannot be created or destroyed, only transformed. Spiritually, this mirrors eternity. The animating force within you does not vanish. It transitions.

Kinetic energy is movement. Every heartbeat, every ocean wave, every step forward. Spiritually, it reflects flow. When you resist growth, you stagnate. When you move in faith and alignment, life unfolds.

Potential energy is power waiting to be expressed. It is the quiet possibility inside you before action begins. Spiritually, it mirrors divine potential. The Creator's power resting within creation. This is where masculine and feminine balance becomes essential. Structure without intuition stalls potential. Intuition without action leaves potential dormant. Balance activates it.

Electromagnetic energy includes light, sound, and radio waves. Invisible yet undeniably real. Thoughts function similarly. They transmit. They resonate. Jesus said, "It is done unto you as you believe." That is energetic law.

Chemical energy transforms food into life force. Scientists remind us that the atoms in our bodies originated in stars. You are not separate from the cosmos. You are stardust reorganized by divine intelligence.

Gravitational energy keeps planets in orbit. Spiritually, it represents grounding. The same intelligence that holds galaxies in place holds your body upright. When you stand barefoot on the earth, you reconnect to rhythm. You remember that divine energy is not distant. It is beneath your feet.

Balance is built into creation. Nothing drifts without order.

Emotional Energy and Spiritual Maturity

Emotions are energy in motion. Love expands. Fear contracts. Anger intensifies. Gratitude elevates. When you manage your emotions, you manage your vibration.

There was a season in my life when anger ruled me. My temper was rooted in hurt and fear. I allowed that energy to dictate my behavior. Eventually I realized that while trauma may explain reaction, it does not excuse it. I enrolled in anger management classes. That was the beginning of learning how to guide energy rather than be ruled by it.

Spiritual maturity is not about suppressing emotion. It is about directing it.

If God is divine energy, and we are made in the image of God, then our ability to shift our frequency is part of that image. We are not powerless spectators. We are conscious participants.

Alignment means your inner world matches your outer expression. Your thoughts, emotions, values, and actions move in the same direction. That is energetic integrity.

Raising Vibration

Modern science confirms that everything vibrates. Ancient wisdom already knew this. When you operate in love, gratitude, and peace, your energetic field expands. When you dwell in fear and resentment, it contracts.

This is not mystical exaggeration. It is observable reality.

Two people can face the same situation and respond differently because their inner frequency differs. One sees opportunity. The other sees defeat. The outer world mirrors the inner vibration.

If God is infinite energy, then connecting with God is less about posture and more about alignment. Prayer, meditation, music, sunlight, laughter, silence, these are not empty rituals. They are tools for tuning frequency.

God is not confined to masculine identity. God is the intelligent field of love that responds to alignment.

Money as Energy

Money is another misunderstood form of energy. The word currency comes from current, a flowing movement. Money is not evil. It is neutral until directed.

When I began to understand money as energy rather than possession, my relationship with it changed. I stopped chasing it and started aligning with gratitude. I bless money when I receive it. I thank God for provision before spending it. That gratitude keeps energy circulating.

Abundance is not only financial. It is peace of mind. It is restored relationships. It is health after surgery. It is laughter with children. It is waking up grounded and grateful.

If God is Source, then money is not the source. It is simply one channel through which divine provision flows.

Divine Energy and Divine Image

At the core of everything, beneath matter and memory, you are light in motion. You are spiritual electricity animated by divine intelligence. If we are created in the image of God, and if God is infinite energy, then that image cannot be male alone.

Masculine and feminine energies are expressions within the field, not definitions of it.

When you operate in strength to protect your children, that is divine energy. When you soften to comfort them, that is divine energy. When you build a business with structure and authority, that is divine energy. When you nurture healing in your home, that is divine energy.

God is not a man. God is the infinite intelligence expressing through both.

The Final Realization

Energy never lies. It introduces you before you speak. It shapes rooms before words are exchanged. It flows through you constantly.

You are not separate from divine energy. You are participating in it.

The more you understand that, the less you limit God to a human category. The less you divide yourself into acceptable and unacceptable expressions. The more you live balanced.

Masculine and feminine energies exist within you because they exist within Source.

God is not confined to male form.

God is the eternal, intelligent field of love from which all vibration flows, and you are living, breathing evidence of that truth.

In59Seconds Publishing Co

10

Where Does That Leave Women?

There is a question that has lingered quietly in the hearts of many women for generations, even when it was never spoken out loud. If humanity was created in the image of God, and if God is exclusively male, then where does that leave women in the spiritual hierarchy? That question is not rebellion. It is a logical question. It causes one to reflect. It is the natural consequence of trying to reconcile divine image with lived reality.

From childhood, many women are taught to revere God as Father, Lord, King. Those titles are not inherently harmful. They carry power and protection within their historical context. Yet when every representation of divine authority is masculine, something subtle can begin to form in the subconscious. Authority begins to look male. Ultimate power begins to look male. The face of heaven begins to look male.

Over time, that repetition can quietly suggest that women are reflections of something secondary rather than something original. Even when churches preach equality in spirit, the consistent imagery may tell a different story beneath the surface. When sermons, paintings, leadership structures, and sacred language all reinforce masculinity as divine representation, women may internalize the idea that their likeness to God is indirect rather than direct.

Genesis states that God created humanity in the divine image, male and female. That line is often read quickly and then passed over. Its implications are profound. The verse does not separate divine likeness into two unequal categories. It does not say that one carries more image than the other. It presents both as reflections of the same source.

If God were exclusively male in essence, then woman would represent a derivative creation rather than a co bearer of divine likeness. Yet scripture does not describe woman as spiritually inferior. It describes her as equally created in the image of God. That equality demands that the divine image include qualities expressed through both masculine and feminine embodiment.

History complicates this conversation because societies have often been patriarchal. Leadership structures shaped interpretation. Male dominated institutions naturally elevated masculine imagery. Over centuries, theology absorbed cultural hierarchy. What began as metaphor for authority slowly merged with assumptions about spiritual order.

Acknowledging that does not mean dishonoring scripture. It means recognizing that interpretation always happens through human lenses. When women begin to ask where they fit within divine image, they are not attacking faith. They are seeking coherence. They are seeking dignity. They are seeking alignment between doctrine and lived experience.

The harm has not always been loud. It has often been quiet. It shows up when women feel called to lead but are told authority is not theirs. It appears when spiritual gifts are questioned because of gender. It surfaces when women struggle to see themselves reflected in sacred imagery. That struggle is not about ego. It is about identity.

If divine source contains both the qualities we describe as masculine and feminine, then women are not spiritual afterthoughts. They are not secondary expressions. They are direct reflections of divine nature. Intuition, nurture, creativity, emotional depth, receptivity, these are not lesser traits. They are divine traits. They originate in the same infinite presence that gives rise to strength and structure.

Recognizing this does not diminish men. It restores balance. It affirms that men do not hold exclusive resemblance to God and that women are not required to mimic masculinity in order to feel powerful. When divine image is expanded to include the fullness of both energies, women no longer have to reconcile their identity with limitation.

There is also freedom for men within this expansion. When divine image is no longer confined to stern authority, men are released from the pressure to suppress gentleness. Emotional expression becomes part of divine likeness rather than a departure from it. Both genders benefit from a larger understanding.

Understanding this shifts something internally. It removes subtle inferiority. It quiets unnecessary comparison. It affirms that spiritual authority is not assigned by gender but by alignment. Women do not need permission to recognize their reflection in divine source. It was there from the beginning.

The deeper truth is steady and unshakable. A source that created all humanity cannot exclude half of it from its own nature. If women exist, if feminine energy exists, if intuition and nurture exist, they must originate from divine intelligence.

Women are not standing outside the image of God hoping to be included. They stand within it fully. They have always been inside it.

Where does that leave women You Ask? It leaves them exactly where they have always been. In the image of God.

11

The God Within

After traveling across continents, meditating on top of Mountains in Pure, entering temples and pyramids Egypt, praying in monasteries in Greece and sacred water fountains in Indonesia, I eventually realized something that felt both humbling and simple. The divine presence I had been searching for in distant places had never been distant at all. It was within me.

You do not command your heart to beat, it heart beats without waiting for your permission. While you sleep, oxygen continues to move through your body and blood circulates with quiet precision. No conscious effort of yours directs it, yet everything functions in remarkable order. Long before medicine is applied, the body often begins repairing itself. An intelligence is at work beneath your awareness, steady and consistent. This process is not chaotic or accidental. It operates with structure and purpose, sustaining life moment by moment.

If divine source were distant and detached, this level of internal order would be difficult to explain. The body functions through intricate systems that cooperate flawlessly. Cells regenerate and wounds close all on their own. Breath moves through us rhythmically in and out. Intentional conscious thought is not required for any of it. The intelligence that governs these processes exists beyond us.

Many religious traditions speak of the kingdom of heaven being within. That phrase is often spiritualized and left abstract. When you begin to observe your own body honestly, it becomes tangible. The presence that sustains life is not merely observing you from above. It is animating you from within.

When you begin to see it this way, your relationship with God naturally shifts. Prayer no longer feels like begging something outside of you to intervene. It starts to feel like aligning yourself internally with what is already present and active. Meditation stops being an escape from life and becomes a way of noticing what has been there all along. Even faith changes. Instead of blind belief, it becomes recognition of an intelligence that has been operating within and around you the entire time.

During my years of searching, I encountered countless rituals and symbols designed to honor divine presence. Each had meaning. Each had beauty. Each offered insight. Yet the most profound realization came quietly. The divine source I sought in pyramids, temples, and mountaintops was the same presence regulating my heartbeat.

That realization did not erase reverence for sacred spaces. It deepened it. Sacred places are reminders. They are invitations to awareness. They are physical reflections of something internal. When you stand in a temple and feel peace, you are not borrowing holiness from stone. You are awakening to what already lives within you.

Understanding that God is within does not mean elevating ego. It means recognizing participation. It means acknowledging that divine intelligence flows through you. It means understanding that your thoughts, your emotions, your alignment matter because they interact with universal law.

Universal law operates whether acknowledged or not. Gravity functions consistently. Kindness produces atmosphere. Bitterness produces tension. Actions yield consequence. These are not punishments. They are patterns embedded in existence.

When you realize that divine presence is within and that universal laws govern reality, responsibility replaces arrogance. Blame becomes less appealing. Judgment softens. You begin to understand that it truly is done unto you as you believe. Thought shapes perception. Perception influences behavior. Behavior influences outcome.

Believing that there is a divine presence within you changes the way you carry yourself through the world. It restores dignity in places where shame once lived. Instead of seeing yourself as small and helpless, waiting for rescue from something outside of you, you begin to recognize that the very intelligence sustaining your breath is already at work within your life. That realization softens desperation and replaces it with steadiness. You are no longer pleading from a place of emptiness. You are aligning with a presence that has never left you.

Alignment, however, is not automatic. It asks something of you, and it calls for honesty about your fears and your habitual patterns. It invites gratitude for what is already functioning in your favor, even when circumstances feel uncertain. Humility becomes a natural response, not because you feel insignificant, but because you recognize that life itself is operating through a wisdom greater than your ego. Awareness begins to grow quietly as you begin to notice how often you have underestimated the strength already inside you.

Once you understand that the capacity to build a meaningful and peaceful life lives within you, there is no returning to the old way of thinking. That knowledge changes how you respond to difficulty. Challenges no longer appear as proof of abandonment. They become invitations to remember who you are connected to. When you know that divine intelligence is not distant but present, you stop collapsing at every obstacle. You stand confidently and begin to think differently.

My own search for truth took me through different teachings, different environments, and different interpretations of God. I explored structure and I explored freedom. What surprised me most was that the farther I traveled intellectually and spiritually, the more I was led back to something simple. There is a divine source governing existence, and it is not fragile. It does not shrink when it is questioned. There is no need for it to get defensive. It does not belong to one culture, one gender, or one denomination. It is All and within every one of us.

That source cannot be boxed into masculine or feminine language alone. It expresses strength and tenderness. It embodies authority and compassion. It holds structure and intuition in beautiful perfect balance. The more I allowed myself to expand my understanding, the more peaceful my faith became. I no longer felt pressured to defend an image of God. I felt invited to deepen my own awareness.

Recognizing the God within you does not make you arrogant. It makes you responsible and wise. If divine intelligence operates through you, then your thoughts and your choices matter. The way you treat others matters. You begin to see your life not as something happening randomly, but as something unfolding through your own conscious participation. Prayer becomes conversation. Reflection becomes communion. Daily living becomes sacred ground that you control.

Here is the truth that changes everything: the presence you have been searching for has never been far away. It has been steady in your breathing, patient in your growth, and quiet in your moments of prayer, meditation and clarity. It is alive, sustaining you even now. The divine is not distant, and it is not fragile. It is closer than you were ever taught to believe, and powerful enough to guide you when you finally choose to recognize it.

12

Living in Balanced Power

Understanding divine masculine and feminine energy is one thing. Living in balance with those energies is something entirely different. Knowledge feels empowering in the moment, but real life is where integration is tested. The real question is not whether you believe God contains both male and female expressions. The real question is whether you allow yourself to express both without fear.

Balanced power is not loud. It does not require a dramatic performance. Nor does it need to prove itself in every room. It feels grounded, steady, and aware. When someone is living in balance, there is a sense of internal order that does not depend on external validation. Your decisions are made with clarity rather than reaction. Emotions are felt without being allowed to control your behavior. You can be authoritative without being harsh. You can also be compassionate without being weak.

Many of us were raised in environments that praised one energy while quietly discouraging the other. Men were often encouraged to lead, build, conquer, and suppress vulnerability. Women were often encouraged to nurture, soften, support, and avoid confrontation. Those patterns became embedded not only in family structures but also in religious interpretation. Divine authority was portrayed as masculine, while tenderness was sometimes treated as secondary or sentimental.

When you begin to see God as the union of both energies, something inside you relaxes. You no longer feel the pressure to fit yourself into a narrow spiritual mold. A woman can lead without apologizing for her strength. A man can feel deeply without questioning his identity. Both can operate in power without feeling fragmented.

Living in balanced power begins with awareness. It requires asking yourself whether your current patterns are aligned or reactive. When you find yourself pushing aggressively to be heard, it may be masculine energy disconnected from compassion. When you find yourself avoiding necessary confrontation to keep the peace, it may be feminine energy disconnected from structure. Neither response makes you flawed. It simply indicates that balance has shifted.

In leadership, balanced power looks like decisiveness tempered by empathy. You can make firm decisions without humiliating others. You can hold standards without becoming rigid. You can enforce boundaries without shutting down connection. Authority rooted in love carries a different weight than authority rooted in ego.

In relationships, balanced power allows both partners to move fluidly between initiative and receptivity. Sometimes one person provides structure while the other nurtures growth. At other times, those roles reverse. Healthy relationships are not rigidly assigned. They are responsive. When both individuals understand they carry both energies, competition decreases and cooperation increases.

Parenting offers another example. A child requires discipline and direction. That is masculine energy functioning properly. The same child also requires warmth, emotional presence, and reassurance. That is feminine energy functioning properly. When one is present without the other, imbalance appears. Discipline without love creates fear. Love without boundaries creates chaos.

Spiritual practice itself reflects this balance. Structured prayer, scripture study, ritual, and discipline represent masculine energy. Meditation, reflection, surrender, and intuition represent feminine energy. A spiritual life built solely on structure can become rigid and legalistic. A spiritual life built solely on emotional flow can become ungrounded. Balance brings depth.

Balanced power also changes how you view success. In many cultures, success has been defined almost exclusively through masculine traits: achievement, accumulation, dominance, and visibility. Feminine expressions such as collaboration, intuition, emotional intelligence, and relational depth were often undervalued. As understanding evolves, people are beginning to recognize that sustainable success requires both.

A business that values structure but ignores emotional health will experience burnout. A business that values creativity but ignores discipline will struggle with stability. The same principle applies to personal growth. Structure without softness exhausts the soul. Softness without structure stalls momentum.

Learning to live in balanced power means giving yourself permission to adjust in real time. There will be moments when firmness is necessary. There will be moments when gentleness is required. Wisdom lies in sensing which energy the moment calls for rather than reacting from habit.

Many people struggle because they identify too strongly with one expression. A woman who prides herself on independence may resist receiving support because receptivity feels vulnerable. A man who identifies strongly with emotional sensitivity may avoid taking initiative because direction feels uncomfortable. Neither tendency is wrong. Both become limiting when they are rigid.

Divine balance invites flexibility. It allows you to shift without losing yourself. You can be assertive without becoming aggressive. You can be compassionate without becoming passive. You can lead without overpowering. You can yield without disappearing.

As you begin to live this way, confidence grows quietly. It does not rely on comparison. It does not rely on dominance. It does not rely on being the loudest voice. Balanced confidence feels anchored because it draws from both stability and intuition.

Another transformation occurs when judgment softens. Understanding that everyone carries both energies allows you to view others with more grace. A man expressing tenderness is no longer perceived as weak. A woman expressing authority is no longer perceived as intimidating. These expressions are seen as whole rather than threatening.

Balanced power also deepens humility. When you recognize that universal law governs outcomes, arrogance loses its appeal. Actions carry consequences. Thoughts influence perception. Kindness creates atmosphere. Cruelty creates tension. These laws operate consistently, just like gravity. You cannot override them with ego.

Living in alignment with these principles simplifies life. Be kind if you desire kindness. Speak truth if you desire trust. Act with integrity if you desire stability. Show love if you desire love returned. The formulas are not complicated, even though ego often complicates them.

One of the most powerful shifts that occurs when living in balanced power is the release of comparison. Comparison thrives in imbalance because it measures dominance. Balance eliminates the need to compete spiritually. Your path to God does not invalidate someone else's. Your method of prayer does not cancel another's devotion. Respect becomes natural when you understand that divine presence is larger than any single expression.

When you have traveled across continents and witnessed countless ways people honor God, it becomes easier to see that diversity does not threaten truth. It enriches it. Balanced power does not need to convert everyone. It needs only to live authentically.

This authenticity produces peace. You stop arguing to defend your belief because you are no longer insecure about it. You stop judging other paths because you recognize that divine intelligence responds to alignment more than to labels. Humility replaces superiority.

Living in balanced power also transforms how you speak to yourself. Harsh internal criticism is often masculine energy distorted into self aggression. Chronic self doubt is often feminine energy distorted into insecurity. Balanced inner dialogue combines accountability with compassion. You can correct yourself without condemning yourself. You can extend grace without excusing harmful behavior.

The more you practice this integration, the more stable you feel. Life will still bring challenges. People will still misunderstand you. Circumstances will still shift. Balance does not eliminate difficulty. It strengthens resilience.

Resilience rooted in balance is powerful because it is not brittle. Rigidity breaks under pressure. Fluidity adapts. When masculine stability and feminine adaptability work together, you can face uncertainty without collapsing.

This integration ultimately reflects divine nature more accurately than either extreme. A God who contains both energies would not operate from imbalance. A God who governs through both structure and compassion would not demand that humanity suppress half of itself.

Living in balanced power is not about perfection. It is about awareness and adjustment. There will be days when you lean too far into one expression. Recognizing that is growth. Correcting gently is wisdom.

The freedom that comes with integration is profound. You no longer feel trapped by expectations placed on your gender. You no longer feel confused when you express qualities that defy stereotypes. You begin to see yourself as whole rather than divided.

When wholeness becomes your foundation, your relationship with God transforms again. Prayer feels like alignment rather than pleading. Meditation feels like tuning into a frequency that has always been present. Faith feels like cooperation with universal law rather than fear of punishment.

Balanced power allows you to honor God in a way that uplifts you while respecting how others honor God in ways that uplift them. That respect is not relativism. It is humility. It acknowledges that divine intelligence is not threatened by human diversity.

Living this way feels steady. It feels adult. It feels mature. It feels spiritually grounded rather than spiritually anxious.

When you understand that God is not limited to one gender, and that you carry both expressions within you, your identity expands. Power stops being something you chase externally. It becomes something you steward internally, and when you live from that place, your presence alone becomes balanced.

#In59Seconds

13

The Symbol of Balance

Long before modern spiritual language began using the terms divine masculine and divine feminine, ancient cultures had already found ways to illustrate balance visually. One of the most recognized symbols in the world is the yin and yang. At first glance, it appears simple. A circle divided into black and white, each side containing a small dot of the other. Yet that simplicity carries depth that aligns perfectly with what this book has been unfolding.

The yin and yang symbol does not represent opposition. It represents interdependence. The black contains white. The white contains black. Neither exists independently. Neither is superior. The symbol communicates movement, rhythm, and relationship rather than hierarchy. That is the key. It does not suggest that one side conquers the other. It suggests that harmony exists only when both are acknowledged.

Yin is often associated with receptive, intuitive, inward, nurturing energy. Yang is associated with active, assertive, outward, directive energy. Those descriptions closely mirror what many now call feminine and masculine expressions. The ancient Chinese philosophers who developed this symbol understood something fundamental about life. Everything moves in cycles. Everything contains polarity. Health is not found in eliminating one side. It is found in balancing both.

The circle itself matters. It communicates wholeness. There is no break in the shape. No edge that separates one side from existence. The energies flow into one another. This visual reinforces a truth that applies directly to humanity. No person is purely one expression. Even in our strongest moments of structure and decisiveness, intuition operates quietly beneath the surface. Even in our deepest moments of compassion and softness, strength is present.

Modern psychology confirms what ancient symbols illustrated. Studies in neuroscience show that emotional intelligence and logical reasoning are not separate systems competing for control. They operate through interconnected neural networks. The prefrontal cortex, responsible for planning and decision making, works in constant communication with the limbic system, which processes emotion. Healthy decision making requires both. When one dominates unchecked, imbalance appears.

Research in leadership studies also supports this integration. Organizations led by individuals who combine assertiveness with empathy consistently outperform those led by rigid, authoritarian figures. A 2016 study published in the Harvard Business Review found that leaders who demonstrate emotional intelligence alongside decisiveness build stronger team trust and long term stability. Structure without empathy increases turnover. Empathy without structure decreases clarity. Balanced leadership sustains growth.

These findings are not separate from spirituality. They reflect it. Universal law expresses itself in both visible and invisible systems.

Life occasionally forces us into intense expressions of one energy. Consider the mother whose child is trapped beneath a fallen tree. In that moment, adrenaline floods her system. Strength surges. Muscles respond with force she may never have known she possessed. Society might label that masculine energy because it resembles raw physical power and protection. Yet that strength is activated by love. It is feminine nurture expressed through masculine force. The separation dissolves when survival and devotion intersect.

Human beings are capable of remarkable shifts depending on circumstance. A man who appears firm and structured at work may become deeply tender when holding his newborn child. A woman who moves gently through daily life may become fiercely authoritative when defending her family. These moments are not contradictions. They are demonstrations of integrated capacity.

Extreme imbalance, however, produces dysfunction. Research in psychology has shown that rigid adherence to traditional gender stereotypes correlates with higher levels of stress and internal conflict. A 2015 study in the Journal of Counseling Psychology found that individuals who felt pressured to conform strictly to gender norms experienced increased anxiety and reduced psychological well being. The internal tension between authentic expression and social expectation creates strain.

Balance reduces that strain. When people allow themselves access to the full spectrum of their emotional and behavioral range, resilience increases. Studies on adaptive coping mechanisms reveal that individuals who combine problem solving strategies with emotional processing recover from stress more effectively than those who rely on only one approach. Problem solving reflects structured energy. Emotional processing reflects intuitive energy. Healing requires both.

The yin and yang symbol also contains an important detail that many overlook. Each side holds a small circle of the other. Within strength lives softness. Within softness lives strength. That detail dismantles the illusion that one energy can exist in isolation. Attempting to eliminate one side creates instability. Attempting to suppress emotion leads to emotional outbursts later. Attempting to suppress strength leads to resentment.

Cultural history provides countless examples of imbalance. Societies that leaned heavily into domination and conquest often collapsed under their own rigidity. Communities that lacked structure struggled with sustainability. Balance is not simply personal. It is collective.

Spiritual traditions across continents have echoed this principle in different language. Ancient Egyptian cosmology emphasized Ma'at, the concept of cosmic balance and order. Greek philosophy spoke of the golden mean, the virtue that exists between extremes. Indigenous traditions honor harmony with nature rather than dominance over it. The language changes. The principle remains steady.

In modern life, imbalance shows up in subtle ways. Hustle culture glorifies relentless productivity, often neglecting rest and reflection. Emotional avoidance is sometimes praised as strength, even though unprocessed emotion eventually surfaces. On the other side, constant introspection without action can lead to stagnation. Movement requires intention. Intention requires clarity. Clarity requires both reasoning and intuition working together.

Living balanced does not mean you will never operate intensely in one expression. There will be seasons that demand firm leadership. There will be seasons that require deep emotional presence. The key lies in returning to center once the moment has passed. Remaining in survival mode when survival is no longer required creates distortion.

The human nervous system illustrates this beautifully. The sympathetic nervous system activates fight or flight responses. The parasympathetic nervous system restores calm and healing. Both are necessary. Constant activation of one leads to burnout. Health depends on oscillation between the two. Balance is biological.

When applied spiritually, this oscillation becomes conscious. You may pray fervently in one season and sit in silent meditation in another. You may lead boldly in one moment and surrender gracefully in another. Neither expression diminishes the other. Both reflect wholeness.

The more humanity studies psychology, biology, and social systems, the clearer it becomes that rigid extremes are unsustainable. Balanced individuals demonstrate higher emotional regulation, stronger interpersonal relationships, and greater life satisfaction. A 2020 meta analysis on emotional regulation strategies found that individuals who integrate both cognitive reappraisal and emotional acceptance report lower stress levels and improved mental health outcomes. Again, structure and feeling operating together.

The spiritual implication is profound. If divine source expresses both energies in harmony, then living in balance aligns you with divine nature more accurately than clinging to one side. Excessive dominance, excessive passivity, excessive aggression, excessive avoidance, all signal misalignment.

The yin and yang symbol remains powerful because it reminds us visually that opposites are not enemies. They are partners. Light requires darkness to be seen. Activity requires rest to be sustained. Expansion requires contraction to remain stable.

Balance is not passive. It requires attention. It requires honesty about where you may be leaning too heavily. It requires the humility to adjust without shame.

Human beings are dynamic. Circumstances will call forth different expressions. Strength may surge when protection is needed. Gentleness may surface when healing is required. Neither defines you entirely. Integration defines you.

The deeper lesson is not about gender at all. It is about wholeness. Masculine and feminine language provides a framework, but the essence is unity within polarity. The symbol teaches that the goal is not elimination of one side but alignment of both.

When you learn to live this way, internal conflict decreases. You stop fighting parts of yourself. You stop judging others for expressing qualities differently than you would. You begin to see balance as strength rather than compromise.

That understanding reinforces the central truth of this book. A divine source capable of creating complexity would not operate from imbalance. If we are reflections of that source, then integration is not optional. It is essential.

Living balanced does not make you weak. It makes you stable, and stability is power.

In59Seconds Publishing Co

14

Spiritual Maturity in a Growing World

There comes a point in every person's life when inherited belief must become examined belief. Childhood faith often begins with trust in what we are told. Adult faith requires internal confirmation. That shift is not a betrayal of upbringing. It is the natural progression of spiritual maturity.

Humanity itself is undergoing a similar shift. Information travels faster than ever before. Cultures interact in ways that were once impossible. People can witness how others worship, pray, meditate, and honor the divine without leaving their homes. Exposure does not automatically produce wisdom, but it does remove isolation. When isolation fades, certainty often softens.

Spiritual maturity is not about abandoning what you were taught. It is about understanding why you believe what you believe. There is a difference between inherited conviction and integrated conviction. Inherited conviction defends itself aggressively because it has never been examined. Integrated conviction remains steady because it has been tested.

As more people travel, read ancient texts, explore global traditions, and observe the diversity of spiritual expression across continents, it becomes harder to maintain the assumption that one cultural lens contains the entire picture. That realization does not require rejecting faith. It requires humility.

Humility is the quiet recognition that divine truth is larger than personal interpretation.

Throughout history, religious institutions have often felt threatened by expansion. Questions have been labeled dangerous. Exploration has been discouraged. Yet questioning has always been part of spiritual growth. The Psalms are filled with questions. The prophets wrestled with doubt. Even Jesus asked why he felt forsaken. Inquiry does not weaken faith. It refines it.

When someone begins to step outside the boundaries of what they were taught in order to seek deeper understanding, fear often follows. Fear of being wrong. Fear of disappointing family. Fear of spiritual consequences. Yet sincere search motivated by a desire for truth is not rebellion against God. It is movement toward understanding.

Spiritual maturity recognizes that God does not require fragility. A divine source capable of creating galaxies is not threatened by honest curiosity. If truth is truly divine, it can withstand examination.

As humanity evolves, conversations about gender, energy, consciousness, and universal law are becoming more open. Some respond with resistance. Others respond with enthusiasm. The balanced position requires discernment rather than reaction. Not every new idea is truth. Not every traditional belief is complete. Maturity involves evaluating both carefully.

The expansion of understanding around masculine and feminine energy is part of this broader evolution. For centuries, imbalance shaped social structures. Power leaned heavily into domination rather than integration. As awareness grows, more people are recognizing the cost of that imbalance. Emotional suppression has led to mental health crises. Authoritarian systems have led to oppression. Hyper passivity has led to stagnation. Extremes reveal their own instability over time.

Spiritual maturity calls for integration rather than polarization. It invites strength with compassion, conviction with humility, belief with openness. It encourages individuals to hold their faith confidently while allowing others the dignity of holding theirs.

When you understand that divine source is not confined to a single gender, denomination, or culture, your posture toward the world changes. You stop needing to prove that your path is superior. You become more interested in living your truth than defending it.

This shift does not produce apathy. It produces responsibility. If it is truly done unto you as you believe, then belief becomes something to steward carefully. Thoughts matter. Intentions matter. Actions matter. Universal law responds consistently.

Spiritual maturity also recognizes that growth never stops. The moment someone declares that they have arrived at complete understanding, stagnation begins. Humility keeps learning alive. It acknowledges that infinite source cannot be fully grasped by finite minds.

The more I traveled, studied, prayed, and reflected, the more I realized that my early image of God was not wrong. It was incomplete. Completion did not require abandonment. It required expansion.

That expansion softened my judgments. It reduced my need to categorize others as right or wrong based solely on terminology. It strengthened my belief in universal law while loosening my attachment to rigid interpretation.

A spiritually mature person can sit in a church and feel reverence. The same person can stand in an ancient temple and feel reverence. The posture of the heart matters more than the architecture of the building.

Growth often feels uncomfortable at first. It stretches mental frame-works. It challenges assumptions. It exposes blind spots. Yet discomfort is not destruction. It is evidence that something is expanding.

The world is changing. Conversations are widening. People are asking deeper questions. Some will cling tightly to familiar boundaries. Others will abandon structure entirely. The balanced path walks between those extremes.

Faith does not need to be narrow to be strong. Strength anchored in humility remains stable. Conviction grounded in compassion remains kind.

Spiritual maturity is the ability to hold complexity without losing center.

It is knowing what you believe and why you believe it.

It is respecting that others may arrive at different conclusions without feeling threatened.

It is understanding that divine source is too vast to be fully contained in any single image.

And it is trusting that sincere search, grounded in love and integrity, will always lead toward greater clarity rather than away from it.

This chapter prepares us for the final step. Integration is complete.

Now we close with power.

In59Seconds Publishing Co

15

Coming Home to Wholeness

By the time you reach this final chapter, you have walked through history, theology, culture, travel, symbol, psychology, and lived experience. You have examined inherited images. You have considered ancient wisdom. You have reflected on masculine and feminine energy, on imbalance, on universal law, on spiritual maturity. Now it is time to bring everything home.

At its core, this book was never just about theology. It was about freedom. It was about releasing the quiet pressure so many people carry without even realizing it. The pressure to fit into a spiritual mold that feels incomplete. The pressure to express only one side of themselves. The pressure to apologize for strength or to suppress softness.

Freedom begins when you understand that wholeness was always available to you.

There were seasons in my own life when I had no choice but to operate in intense masculine energy. After my divorce, survival was not theoretical. It was immediate. Children needed stability. Bills needed to be paid. Businesses needed to be built from nothing. There was no luxury of waiting for someone else to rescue me. Authority had to be claimed. Decisions had to be made. Discipline had to be maintained.

In those years, I was direct. Focused. Assertive. Structured. I was not trying to prove anything. I was trying to survive and protect what mattered most. Society has a way of criticizing women who operate in that space. Words like aggressive or unfeminine are thrown around casually. Advice is offered about softening and calming down, often by people who have never had to carry the weight of full responsibility alone.

What many fail to understand is that strength activated by necessity is not a rejection of femininity. It is an expression of love.

A mother protecting her children will access power she did not know she possessed. A woman building stability from nothing will tap into structure and authority because life demands it. That does not erase her softness. It reveals her capacity.

As the years passed and survival became stability, I learned something else. Balance is not automatic. After operating in intense strength for so long, softening required intention. I had to remind myself that the world was no longer an emergency. I had to allow tenderness back into spaces that had once required armor. I had to rediscover rest without feeling guilty for it.

Being a boss at work and a loving, present mother at home required conscious shifting. Structure did not need to dominate every room. Authority did not need to define every conversation. Strength could exist alongside warmth. Boundaries could exist alongside affection. It was not about abandoning masculine energy. It was about integrating it with feminine flow.

Many people feel shame when they recognize they are operating in extremes. A man may feel embarrassed by his emotional intensity. A woman may feel judged for her ambition. Yet extremes often emerge from necessity or unhealed experience. They are not proof of failure. They are signals that something has been overused or undernourished.

Life will occasionally require extreme expressions. Crisis demands decisiveness. Protection demands force. Grief demands surrender. Healing demands vulnerability. The key is not to eliminate intensity. The key is to return to center once the moment has passed.

You are not defined by the energy you accessed during survival.

You are defined by your willingness to rebalance when survival is no longer necessary.

This is where grace enters the conversation.

Grace allows you to look back at former versions of yourself without embarrassment. The woman who was sharp and guarded may have been doing exactly what she needed to do at that time. The man who shut down emotionally may have been protecting himself the only way he knew how. Judgment does not heal imbalance. Awareness does.

Recenter yourself as many times as necessary.

There is no spiritual penalty for adjusting.

One of the greatest gifts of understanding divine balance is the release of comparison. You no longer measure your worth by how well you perform masculinity or femininity according to someone else's expectations. You measure alignment by internal peace. When strength feels grounded and not aggressive, you are aligned. When softness feels secure and not fearful, you are aligned.

Divine source does not shame you for expressing strength. Divine source does not shame you for expressing tenderness. Both originate in the same infinite intelligence. If God contains both, then accessing both is not betrayal. It is reflection.

The more you accept this, the more comfortable you become in your own skin.

Comfort does not mean complacency. It means authenticity. It means you can walk into a room without calculating how you need to perform. It means you can speak firmly without fearing that you have compromised your femininity. It means you can show emotion without fearing that you have compromised your masculinity.

This internal comfort radiates outward. Relationships shift. Work environments shift. Children raised by balanced adults learn that strength and gentleness are not enemies. They learn that authority can coexist with kindness. They learn that identity is not confined to stereotype.

Understanding that God is not a man is not about arguing theology. It is about expanding image. When divine source is no longer confined to one gender, you are no longer confined either. You stop asking whether you are allowed to embody certain qualities. You begin asking whether those qualities are balanced and healthy.

Balance will not look the same for everyone. Some people naturally lean toward structure. Others naturally lean toward intuition. Personal temperament plays a role. Cultural background plays a role. Life experience plays a role. What matters is not equal expression at every moment. What matters is access.

Can you access softness when necessary?

Can you access strength when necessary?

If the answer is yes, you are whole.

Universal law remains steady throughout all of this. Actions carry consequences. Belief shapes experience. Kindness yields different outcomes than cruelty. Integrity stabilizes life. These principles do not change based on gender or denomination. They respond to alignment.

It truly is done unto you as you believe.

When you believe you are incomplete, you operate from lack. When you believe you are whole, you operate from sufficiency. When you believe that divine source lives within you, you stop seeking validation from external approval. When you believe that divine image includes both masculine and feminine expression, you stop dividing yourself internally.

Coming home to wholeness feels quiet.

It does not need applause.

It does not need argument.

It feels like exhaling after holding your breath for years.

It feels like realizing you were never missing anything.

The woman who built businesses out of necessity can rest in her softness without losing her authority. The man who led with firmness can rediscover tenderness without losing respect. Both can exist in the same person. Both can exist in harmony.

Your life will continue to call forth different expressions. There will be seasons that demand resilience. There will be seasons that invite surrender. The invitation is not to perfect balance in every moment. The invitation is to remain aware.

Awareness is power.

When you drift too far into dominance, you will feel it. When you drift too far into passivity, you will feel it. That discomfort is not condemnation. It is guidance. Recenter. Adjust. Continue.

Divine source is not fragile. Your identity is not fragile. Growth does not offend God. Balance honors God.

As you close this book, let something settle inside you. Let the pressure to fit into someone else's definition of strength fall away. Let the quiet shame that may have followed you during seasons of intensity dissolve. The strength that carried you through survival was sacred. The softness that returned when safety came back into your life is sacred too. Neither one cancels the other.

There is no apology required for becoming powerful when life demanded it. There is no apology required for reclaiming tenderness when the storm passed. Both expressions were part of your growth. Both were reflections of the divine intelligence that lives within you.

The truth is larger than any narrow image we inherited. Divine source is not confined to gender, personality, or tradition. It is vast, living, and present. If you were created in that image, then wholeness belongs to you. Strength belongs to you. Compassion belongs to you. Authority and gentleness were never meant to compete inside you.

Stand comfortably in who you are becoming. Re-center when necessary and adjust without shame. Lead with strength and power when the moment calls for it and soften with love and compassion when it is needed. The balance is yours to take charge of. Walk forward knowing that nothing about your desire for understanding offends God.

16

Conclusion

The Fullness of Divine Image

This journey was never about winning an argument. It was never about dismantling faith or replacing one tradition with another. It was about expansion. It was about allowing divine image to grow larger in your understanding so that you could grow larger within yourself.

When God is confined to a single gender, something inside humanity contracts. When divine source is expanded to include the fullness of masculine and feminine expression, something inside humanity relaxes. The pressure to perform fades. The quiet tension between strength and softness dissolves. Identity stops feeling like a negotiation.

You were never meant to divide yourself in order to be acceptable to God. You were never meant to suppress half of your nature to fit someone else's theology. The presence that created galaxies, oceans, breath, and bone does not operate in fragments. It operates in wholeness.

Life will still require courage. It will still require structure, discipline, and resilience. There will be seasons when your strength must rise quickly and without hesitation. There will also be seasons that require surrender, patience, empathy, and emotional depth. Neither expression makes you more or less spiritual. Both are reflections of the same divine source moving through you in different forms.

The more you understand this, the less you judge yourself. The more you understand this, the less you judge others. Spiritual arrogance begins to fade because you realize that no single tradition, culture, or gender holds exclusive ownership over the image of God. Reverence becomes deeper when it is no longer restricted by fear.

A balanced life does not happen by accident. It happens through awareness. It happens through the willingness to pause and ask whether you are operating from survival or from stability. It happens through the courage to soften when you no longer need armor and the courage to stand firm when love requires protection.

This understanding brings gratitude. Gratitude for the grandmother who raised you in church. Gratitude for the traditions that sustained you during dark seasons. Gratitude for the travels, the questions, the doubts, the discoveries. Gratitude for the realization that the divine presence you sought in distant lands was also regulating your heartbeat the entire time.

There is something profoundly comforting about knowing that divine source is not limited, not fragile, not offended by sincere exploration. The God you honor is not confined to a single image. The God you honor is vast enough to hold strength and tenderness, authority and compassion, discipline and mercy.

You are made in that image.

That means you are not broken when you lead boldly. You are not broken when you feel deeply. You are not out of alignment when life demands intensity. You are not less spiritual when you reclaim softness. Balance is not perfection. It is conscious returning.

The world does not need more rigid certainty. It needs grounded humility. It needs people who can hold conviction without hostility. It needs women who understand their strength without apologizing for it. It needs men who embrace their emotional depth without questioning their worth. It needs human beings who recognize that divine image was never meant to be divided.

As you move forward, let your faith feel expansive rather than confined. Let your understanding of God reflect infinity rather than limitation. Let your identity feel integrated rather than split.

There is an amazing divine source sustaining existence at every moment. That source is not a man. It is not a woman. It is not confined to language. It is living, intelligent, and present. It is within you and beyond you at the same time.

Rest in that truth. Live from that truth and allow your life to reflect the fullness of the image you were created in.

Also by SaBrina Fisher Reece

SaBrina Fisher Reece was once known throughout California as "The Braid Queen." For more than twenty-six years, she owned and operated the legendary Braids By SaBrina, a celebrated salon and school on Adams Boulevard in Los Angeles. It grew into the largest and most influential braiding establishment in the city, where artistry, empowerment, discipline, and community came together in powerful ways. Her success was entirely self-made, built through perseverance, resilience, and vision, often without consistent external support or validation.

As she stepped into the second half of her life, SaBrina felt a deeper calling unfolding within her. The story behind her success was not just one of entrepreneurship, but one of faith, healing, self-trust, and spiritual awakening. Early experiences of abandonment and profound personal loss led her inward, where she began the real work of emotional healing and inner mastery. What started as creative expression evolved into purposeful transformation.

Today, SaBrina writes self-help books rooted in emotional healing, personal growth, and spiritual awareness. Blending lived experience with motivational insight and metaphysical understanding, she explores themes of balance, resilience, self-mastery, and the unseen forces that shape human thought and behavior. Through her writing and motivational speaking, she guides readers toward deeper self-awareness, renewed confidence, and lives that feel intentional and aligned from the inside out.

She is the author of numerous self-help and transformational works, including *My Spiritual Smile*, *Kicking Depression In the Butt*, *Your Mind Is Magic*, *Perfectly Positive*, *Living Life on a Higher Freequency*, *Spiritual Balance*, *Angry World*, *Become Your Own Cheerleader*, *Self Sabotage*, *How to Get Exactly What You Want From God*, *When I Say "I Am"*, and the popular

Ebooks: *Imagine: Learn How to Use Your Imagination to Design the Life You Desire, You're Not Religious -You're Spiritual-I Get It: Bridging the Gap Between the Two, Take A Breath With Bri: The Power of Intentional Breathing, Is This Why They Burned The Books?: Buried Wisdom From The Past.*

Her passion for sound and frequency has led her to explore the healing power of crystal sound bowls, tuning forks, and flow chimes, tools designed to help harmonize the body, mind, and spirit. Now residing in the enchanting landscapes of New Mexico, "The Land of Enchantment," she offers Sound Vibration Sessions that invite others to slow down, breathe deeply, and reconnect with their higher selves. While she embraces these modalities, she reminds her students and readers that there is no single path to peace. Every journey is sacred, and every sincere method of connecting with the Divine carries value.

Above all, SaBrina is a devoted mother of four, Justin, Joi, Jayden, and Journey, and a proud grandmother to Raiden Jesse and Rio Jordan. Watching them, and those she teaches, awaken to their divine potential remains her greatest joy.

Her message is simple and enduring: we are each born with divine energy, a God-given power to create, to heal, and to live fully. The goal is not perfection, but peace. The journey is not to escape life, but to embrace it, to use positive tools to take control of the mind and become the master of your fate.

Take a Breath with Bri

What if the one thing you've been doing your entire life... is the one thing you've never truly learned to do?

You breathe every single day. Over 20,000 times. Yet most of those breaths happen unconsciously, shallow and rushed, mirroring a world that rarely slows down.

In *Take a Breath With Bri*, motivational speaker Bri Reece invites you to rediscover the most powerful, accessible tool you already possess: your breath.

For decades, Bri lived a fast-paced life, running a business for over thirty years without ever pausing to understand the importance of intentional breathing. It wasn't until her fifties that she slowed down long enough to realize that breath is more than survival. It is regulation. It is clarity. It is peace. It is power.

Blending science, spirituality, and personal experience, this uplifting and deeply personal guide explores:

The medical benefits of slow, controlled breathing

How breath regulates anger, anxiety, and emotional overwhelm

Why impulsive reactions can destroy lives — and how one conscious breath can prevent it

Ancient breathing wisdom from Egypt, India, Tibet, the Andes, and beyond

Simple, practical breathing exercises you can begin immediately

How to teach children emotional regulation through breath

The spiritual significance of breath as the life force within us all

Each chapter gently reminds you that before reacting, before speaking, before escalating, you can pause and take one intentional breath.

Bri's signature message, "Take a breath with Bri, and you will see that everything will be all right," has helped thousands regulate their emotions and find calm in moments of chaos. Now, through this book, she teaches you how to create that steadiness for yourself, anytime, anywhere.

This is not a medical manual. It is a life manual.

It is for the parent who wants to model calm.

It is for the young person overwhelmed by anxiety.

It is for the individual who reacts too quickly.

It is for the spiritual seeker.

It is for anyone who is tired of living in survival mode.

Before you reach for anger. Before you reach for pills. Before you reach for regret. Reach for your breath, and watch your life change - one inhale at a time.

Catch and Cast

Catch and Cast: Reversing Negative Thinking Patterns is an empowering guide to taking control of the mind and ending the cycle of unnecessary emotional suffering.

In this deeply personal and compassionate book, self help author SaBrina Fisher Reece introduces a simple yet transformative approach to mental healing. Drawing from her own lived experience with depression, post traumatic stress, abandonment, and loss, she teaches readers how to stop negative thoughts in their tracks and replace them with thoughts that support peace, self worth, and emotional freedom.

At the heart of the book is the Recognize, Reject, Replace system, a practical framework designed to help readers become aware of harmful thought patterns, consciously refuse them, and intentionally choose healthier alternatives. Rather than encouraging suppression or denial of pain, this method emphasizes awareness, choice, and responsibility, allowing healing to unfold without shame or judgment.

Written in a warm, loving, and conversational voice, **Catch and Cast** reassures readers that negative thoughts do not mean they are broken. It shows how the mind, while powerful, does not have to be in control. Through insight, reflection, and daily practice, readers learn that suffering does not have to be permanent and that peace is possible, even after deep trauma.

This book is for anyone who feels trapped by their thoughts, overwhelmed by recurring mental images, or unaware that they have the power to choose what lives in their inner world. It offers hope without false promises and guidance without condemnation.

Catch and Cast reminds readers that while pain may be part of life, prolonged suffering is not. Healing begins in the mind, and the tools to achieve it are already within reach.

Mind Is All

In Mind is All: Manipulating Ideas in a New Direction, SaBrina Fisher Reece explores the mechanics
of thought-how ideas form, how they gain power,
and how they quietly shape decisions, behavior, and
belief. This book focuses less on positivity as a
concept and more on mental leadership: learning
how to consciously guide thought before it guides
you.

Rather than motivating through inspiration alone, this book challenges
readers to examine where their attention goes and why. It offers a
framework for recognizing habitual thinking and deliberately steering
it in a new, more constructive direction.

In this book, you'll learn how to:
   Identify ideas that limit your growth
   Redirect mental momentum instead of fighting it
   Strengthen focus and internal discipline
   Replace unconscious reactions with intentional thought
   Use awareness to influence outcomes and decisions

Mind Is All is about reclaiming authority over your inner world. When
you learn how ideas are formed and sustained, you gain the ability to
reshape them-and in doing so, reshape your experience of life.

This book is for readers ready to think differently, not just feel better.

Sacred not Separate

How Religion and Spirituality Intersect in Modern Life: What if the line between religion and spirituality was never meant to divide us?

In a world where people argue over doctrine, label one another, and separate themselves based on belief systems, *Sacred, Not Separate* offers a deeply personal and unifying perspective. This book is not about choosing sides. It is about bridging them.

Raised in the Christian Church of God in Christ by her grandmother, Bri Reece grew up rooted in faith, gospel music, prayer, and reverence for God. Later, through world travel, personal trauma, spiritual exploration, and profound healing experiences, she encountered meditation, sound healing, breath work, and ancient earth based practices that expanded her understanding of the divine.

Instead of abandoning religion for spirituality, or rejecting spirituality for religion, she discovered something powerful:

They are not enemies. They are expressions. Through raw storytelling and emotional honesty, Bri explores: The illusion of division between church and spiritual practice The power of sound in both gospel worship and sound healing

How trauma can make us vulnerable to spiritual ego

The importance of discernment in both religious institutions and spiritual centers

Breath as the universal bridge between body and spirit Why meditation and prayer are more alike than we think

How belief shapes our lived experience

Why love is the only true spiritual barometer

This book courageously addresses spiritual manipulation, grief, healing, world travel, cultural perspective, and the personal responsibility we all carry in creating peace. It challenges the idea that God belongs to one structure, one language, or one group of people.

If your beliefs make you kinder, they are aligned.

If they make you cruel, something is off. It is that simple.

Sacred, Not Separate is for the person who loves Jesus but also meditates.

For the one who wears a cross and a crystal. For the family member tired of arguing at the dinner table. For the seeker who refuses to be boxed in. This is not a debate. It is a bridge.

If you are ready to embrace unity without losing your foundation, to deepen your faith without shrinking your curiosity, and to live from a place of one God and one love, this book will meet you exactly where you are. The sacred was never separate.

We just forgot.

Spiritual Balance

Aligning Mind, Body, and Energy in Everyday Life
is a grounded, insightful guide for anyone seeking clarity, emotional stability, and deeper alignment in a fast-moving world.

In this book, SaBrina Fisher Reece explores the truth that many people sense but struggle to articulate: life becomes chaotic when our inner energies are out of balance. Drawing from spiritual principles, lived experience, and practical awareness, *Spiritual Balance* breaks down how the mind, body, and energetic self are deeply interconnected-and how neglecting one inevitably affects the others.

This book reframes common spiritual concepts in a way that is accessible, realistic, and applicable to everyday life. Readers will learn that masculine and feminine energies are not tied to gender, but are universal forces present within every person. When these energies are balanced, we experience greater peace, confidence, emotional regulation, and healthier relationships. When they are not, stress, confusion, and emotional exhaustion take over.

Rather than offering abstract philosophy, *Spiritual Balance* provides readers with a new way of understanding themselves. It encourages self-awareness, intentional living, and emotional responsibility without shame or perfectionism. Topics include emotional balance, energetic boundaries, spiritual awareness, self-worth, and the role of unseen forces in shaping our daily experiences.

This book is for readers who know there is more to life than what can be seen, measured, or explained logically, but who also want something practical, grounded, and honest. *Spiritual Balance* meets spirituality where real life happens: in relationships, work, healing, growth, and everyday decisions.

By aligning mind, body, and energy, readers are guided toward a more peaceful, empowered, and intentional way of living, one that honors both the human experience and the spiritual truth beneath it.

Kicking Depression in the Butt

is a raw, faith-infused, and deeply practical guide for anyone who is tired of surviving in silence and ready to reclaim their life.

Drawing from her own lived experiences with trauma, abandonment, loss, and depression, SaBrina Fisher Reece invites readers into an honest conversation about what depression really feels like, and how to fight back. This book does not minimize pain or offer shallow positivity. Instead, it helps readers recognize depression as an internal enemy, interrupt destructive thought cycles, and rebuild their inner world with intention, truth, and daily tools that actually work.

Through personal storytelling, spiritual insight, and mindset-shifting strategies, SaBrina shows readers how to stop identifying with their darkest thoughts and begin designing a life that protects their peace. She addresses the realities of trauma, triggers, boundaries, faith, therapy, medication, and personal responsibility, offering a balanced approach that honors both professional support and inner work.

Kicking Depression in the Butt is for the person who keeps showing up while quietly falling apart. It is for those who smile while suffering, who feel strong on the outside but exhausted on the inside. Most of all, it is a reminder that depression may visit, but it does not get to stay, and it does not get to become your identity.

This book is not about perfection. It's about progress. It's about learning how to fight for your mind, your peace, and your future, one thought, one choice, and one day at a time.

Because as long as you have breath in your body, your story is not over, and you still have the power to kick depression in the butt.

PERFECTLY POSITIVE

How to Stay Positive When Life Is Not Perfect

Perfectly Positive is a guide to remaining centered, steady, and hopeful in a world that often feels anything but peaceful. Through real-life experiences, practical strategies, and grounded spiritual insight, SaBrina Fisher Reece shows you how to rise above daily stress, unexpected setbacks, and limiting thought patterns to build a life rooted in clarity and purpose.

This book is not about pretending life is flawless. It is about developing the discipline to guide your thoughts, strengthen your mindset, and respond to challenges with intention rather than reaction. Positivity is not personality-driven and it is not accidental. It is a skill that can be developed, practiced, and strengthened over time.

Life brings loss, pressure, disappointment, and uncertainty. Some seasons shake your confidence. Others test your patience. What if you could move through all of it with resilience, emotional steadiness, and renewed perspective? This book offers practical tools to help you do exactly that.

Inside these pages, you will learn how to:

Reframe adversity without denying reality

Strengthen emotional resilience

Shift negative thought patterns into productive ones

Maintain peace in environments you cannot control

Happiness is not the result of perfect circumstances. It is created through conscious thought, steady focus, and personal responsibility. Perfectly Positive reminds you that even in an imperfect world, you have the power to shape your internal experience - and that power changes everything.

Making More Money in Today's Market

For Those Who Are Tired of Struggling Financially

If you are tired of working hard but feeling stuck, tired of doing "everything right" yet still worrying about money, or tired of believing that financial freedom is for other people, this book was written for you.

Making more money is not just about strategy. It's about mindset, focus, and expectation. Long before income changes, belief has to shift. This book begins there.

SaBrina Fisher Reece shares her honest perspective on money, success, and prosperity, not from a place of theory, but from lived experience. She has always expected money to flow, and that expectation shaped her decisions, her confidence, and her results. She also understands that many people were never taught to think that way. They were taught to survive, to settle, or to fear financial growth.

This book is not about shaming where you started. It is about showing you how to change your relationship with money so you can experience more ease, stability, and abundance in this lifetime.

Inside these pages, you will learn how to:

Shift the beliefs that quietly limit your income

Understand money as an exchange of value, not struggle

Develop focus in a market full of distraction

Build confidence around earning, charging, and receiving

Stop repeating financial patterns that no longer serve you

Create a mindset that supports growth in today's economy

This is not a get-rich-quick promise. It is a practical, empowering guide to thinking differently about money so your actions can finally produce different results. Whether you want to increase your income, start a business, grow an existing one, or simply feel less stressed about finances, this book meets you where you are and shows you what's possible next.

You do not need permission to want more. You do not need to struggle forever. You can learn to expect better.

Making More Money in Today's Market is an invitation to shift your focus, expand your expectations, and step into a more prosperous future, starting now.

www.ingramcontent.com/pod-product-compliance
Lightning Source LLC
Chambersburg PA
CBHW060956050726
47592CB00003B/1244